AFRICAN GREY PARROTS

Photography

G. Axelrod, courtesy of Jeffrey and Mary Frohock, Aquarius, Ltd., 2190 East Atlantic Blvd., Pompano Beach, FL 33062: 30, 102. Dr. H. R. Axelrod: 25, 27(bottom), 68, 83, 96, 100, 103. J. Daniel: 111. V. Hart: 49. H. V. Lacey: 8, 16, 84, 85. Dr. E. J. Mulawka: back endpapers, 6, 7, 10, 11, 14, 15, 18, 22, 23, 31, 72, 78, 98, 99, 107, 110, 112. F. Nothaft: 54. E. Roloff: 27(top). Courtesy of San Diego Zoo: 19. Dr. W. C. Satterfield: 114, 115, 118, 119, 122, 123. L. Van der Meid: 76, 86, 87, 88, 89. Courtesy of Vogelpark Walsrode: front endpapers, 5, 26, 106.

ISBN 0-87666-833-3

Distributed in the UNITED STATES by T.F.H. Publications, Inc., 211 West Sylvania Avenue, Neptune City, NJ 07753; in CANADA by H & L Pet Supplies Inc., 27 Kingston Crescent, Kitchener, Ontario N2B 2T6; Rolf C. Hagen Ltd., 3225 Sartelon Street, Montreal 382 Quebec; in ENGLAND by T.F.H. (Great Britain) Ltd., 11 Ormside Way, Holmethorpe Industrial Estate, Redhill, Surrey RH1 2PX; in AUSTRALIA AND THE SOUTH PACIFIC by T.F.H. (Australia) Pty. Ltd., Box 149, Brookvale 2100 N.S.W., Australia; in NEW ZEALAND by Ross Haines & Son, Ltd., 18 Monmouth Street, Grey Lynn, Auckland 2 New Zealand; in SINGAPORE AND MALAYSIA by MPH Distributors Pte., 71-77 Stamford Road, Singapore 0617; in the PHILIPPINES by Bio-Research, 5 Lippay Street, San Lorenzo Village, Makati, Rizal; in SOUTH AFRICA by Multipet Pty. Ltd., 30 Turners Avenue, Durban 4001. Published by T.F.H. Publications Inc., Ltd., the British Crown Colony of Hong Kong.

AFRICAN GREY
PARROTS

Dr. Edward J. Mulawka

Amazona ochrocephala oratrix, Amazona aestiva xanthopteryx (center) and *Psittacus erithacus erithacus*. These three parrots are internationally recognized for their mimicry. The African grey, however, stands out from all other parrots because of its unique coloration.

Opposite:
The African grey's unique coloration, its astounding ability to mimic and its apparent intelligence make it highly prized by many bird fanciers.

6

African grey parrot, *Psittacus erithacus*.

Contents

In the minds of many bird fanciers, the double yellow-headed Amazon, *Amazona ochrocephala oratrix*, and the African grey parrot, *Psittacus e. erithacus*, vie for the position of overall favorite parrot.

Opposite:
The African grey is by far the most commonly encountered large African parrot in captivity, and in Europe it is the most popular parrot of all.

Dedication

To the many teachers of my life, especially Dr. August Kerber, who patiently taught me to seek out truth, beauty and joy, and to savor each as if there would be no tomorrow.

E.J.M.

Acknowledgments

I wish to express my gratitude to my many friends and acquaintances who gave me the encouragement, incentive and often sound advice which was needed for the completion of this book.

I particularly wish to thank a number of people who provided me access to birds so that photographs could be taken to illustrate the written material.

Special thanks to the San Diego Zoo for permitting me to photograph *timnehs* from within their flight cage. I sincerely appreciate the gracious generosity of Miss Georgeanne Irvine, public relations officer for the San Diego Zoo, who went to great pains to arrange a photography session. Special thanks also to the Los Angeles Zoo and particularly to the curator of birds, Mr. Michael Cunningham, who made me welcome. I am especially grateful for being permitted to see rare birds generally not available to the public.

It was a pleasure to have the opportunity of visiting Joy Bird Imports of Canoga Park, California, and photographing some Congolese African greys which had just recently been released from quarantine. The cordial and pleasant staff were a pleasure to meet and work with.

Finally, but not at all least, I wish to acknowledge the assistance given me by my friends Helen and Dave Schuelke and their attractive daughter Tracy. It is always a pleasure visiting with them and having the opportunity of seeing the Schuelke Collection of parrots and photographing them.

Psittacus erithacus timneh. This subspecies is somewhat smaller than the nominate subspecies. Note the drab brownish red tail.

Opposite:
Psittacus e. erithacus. Even in the shade, the tail of the nominate subspecies appears a brighter shade of red than that of *P. e. timneh.*

Although African greys have for centuries been kept as pets, there is still much to be learned about the birds' behavior in the wild and in captivity.

Introduction

The African grey is by far one of the most popular of parrot species kept in captivity. Its popularity spans several centuries, and there is even some reason to believe that the species was introduced into Italy during the heyday of imperial Rome. While its popularity as a pet is history and its prowess as a talking bird and household pet is legend, there is, strangely enough, still much to be learned about the species.

The intent of this book is twofold: first, to compile existing ornithological and avicultural data so that some type of composite profile on the species can be developed; second, to provide the student interested in the African grey with some understanding about the creature's habits (both in the wild and in captivity), its breeding cycle and its characteristics as a pet and as a talking bird.

This intent, unfortunately, has been frustrated to some degree, for the profile developed herein is far from complete. While there are numerous references involving the species, usually such sources contain nothing more than a sentence or two—or paragraph or two at best—about the species and its behavior. Much of that information is, moreover, nothing more than a repetition of earlier mentions of the species. Furthermore, particularly in the avicultural publications, articles of exposition on the African grey are sometimes contaminated by hearsay, speculation and contradiction. Data which have been compiled as a result of painstaking observation, research and analysis are difficult to come by in avicultural publications. Succinctly speaking, while there are numerous publications

In the wild, African greys usually prefer to perch in very tall trees.

Opposite:
African greys exhibit a
preference for high places in
captivity as well. This kind of
behavior is typical even for
tamed African greys.

providing elaborate details on a wide variety of animals which are domestically bred for man's consumption and/or pleasure, there is no such concentrated scientific inquiry involving the African grey parrot.

As noted above, one of the tasks of this book is to take the smatterings of information available and to put it into some type of pattern which would form the basis for better understanding the species's behavior and life cycle. There has also been a conscious and deliberate effort to separate the behavior of the wild African grey from that of the captive (and tamed) bird. The reader is well advised, however, to view such a separation with caution.

Unlike the diverse animals which have been selectively bred in order that certain strains exhibiting specific traits could be developed (such as a Labrador Retriever, which has been selectively bred to hone its instincts for retrieving felled wildfowl), African grey parrots have received no specific selective breeding aside from that which occurs in the natural order of evolution. The instinctual patterns of the species and its consequent behavior, therefore, vary insignificantly between wild and captive (tamed) individuals. The tamed parrot differs only in that it tolerates the human presence and even human handling, whereas the wild parrot flees human contact. Since their instinctual patterns of dealing with their environment remain intact and unaltered by genetic engineering, such "tamed" birds will soon revert to wild behavior if left to their own devices. Captivity has the effect of subduing the instinctual patterns characterizing the bird's behavior and nothing more.

Captivity also modifies the species's behavior from the perspective that the creature lives in a totally artificial environment which is predetermined in scope and character by the fancies, desires, imagination and will of the captor. The degree of freedom and movement, and indeed the parrot's very interaction with the captor, is by and large shaped by the manner in which the master interacts with the bird.

It is the master who chooses the conditions under which the bird will become tamed; it is the master who chooses the method of "taming." It is the master who decides which foods will be given the bird, how the bird will be housed and so on.

The captive bird has little freedom to exercise its instincts in such a way as to have an over-all effect on the outcome of its captivity. Nevertheless, while the captive African grey is constrained physically in an environment shaped by the captor and its relationship with man is controlled by man himself, so that for all appearances the wild bird is no longer wild and therefore devoid of instincts, the fact is that the tameness of a pet African grey is simply a veneer. The bird is different from wild individuals in their natural environment only in that the tamed bird has not been allowed to express its natural instincts and that the tolerance of man has been enforced upon it.

This is no less true for captive-bred African grey parrots. While such parrots are usually hand-fed from the time they are two or three weeks old, so that they tend to perceive themselves as "being human," the fact is that such birds are complete with all their natural instincts.

A couple of examples may be useful. Wild African grey parrots choose the highest limbs of the highest trees on which to feed, roost and rest. Captive and tamed birds will also choose the highest point for such activities, given the constraints of their captivity. An acquaintance of mine, to cite another example, purchased a three-month-old African grey which had been hand-fed since its second week. The parrot accompanied the family virtually everywhere. One day while on a camping trip in the mountains surrounding Los Angeles, the parrot simply flew away. It was at the time about three years old. Despite several days of searching, that bird was never again sighted or recovered. In both instances, instincts predominate, and the veneer of tameness reveals itself to be quite shallow.

While the much darker red of the tail feathers most obviously distinguishes *P. e. timneh* from *erithacus*, the gray is darker as well.

Opposite:
Note the scalloped appearance on the breast plumage and the brightly colored red tail of this specimen of *P. e. erithacus*.

This thesis has value toward better understanding the makeup of the species. Tameness is only a condition superimposed on a wild creature, and while it may be helpful to classify behavior into wild and tame, such classifications should be treated with caution. Further, by reminding ourselves that a bird's behavior is a composite of a number of factors and that aspects of its behavior cannot be isolated from the whole, then we may gain better insight on the conditions conducive to successful breeding in captivity.

Some comments may be helpful to the reader concerning the organization of the material. There has been an effort, quite unsatisfactory in many respects, to meld the sciences of ornithology and aviculture into a composite, more or less, and to develop what information that there is in such a manner that it will be useful to the amateur ornithologist, aviculturist and bird fancier. Descriptions of the African grey and its various subspecies have been provided from an ornithological perspective. Again, the reader is cautioned that such physical descriptions are not complete and totally exact. Variations in coloration and size can be found between individual birds, and while such variations do not appear to vary as significantly as is sometimes found in other species of parrots, there are nevertheless variations to be found. Physical descriptions are therefore provided in such terms as will best help the reader to identify the species and its various races.

Further, anatomical features relating to the physiology of the species have been ignored in this text in the belief that such information, while useful to biologists and ornithologists, will be of little value to the type of audience for which this book has been written.

The book is further organized in such a manner as to provide detailed information about the species's behavior in the wild as seen through the eyes of the ornithologist or naturalist on a field expedition. Civilization is rapidly lay-

Although an African grey parrot can be kept in one of the larger cages made especially for parrots, a pet African grey should be allowed to exercise out of its cage as often as possible.

ing waste to the great expanses of wildernesses which stretched across Africa. The natural habitat of the species is being rapidly transformed and altered, with the result that the African grey's behavior and population are being critically affected. Science is fortunate that there is a variety of accounts of observations written about the species during a time when the African landscape remained relatively unscathed. Such reports, especially those of the naturalist and painter Keulemans, provide descriptions of the African grey in conditions that would be difficult to duplicate in today's changed land mass.

Following the ornithological accounts, an examination of the African grey's behavior in captivity is provided. This presentation of the species's behavior is treated from the perspective of the aviculturist and bird fancier. Whenever possible, historical accounts have been drawn upon to provide the reader with those views and experiences of others

Thorough and complete observations of African greys in the wild were first made by J. G. Keulemans.

Opposite:
Typical habitats of the African grey in Sierra Leone (above) and western Africa (below).

27

which best illustrate the species's desirable (and undesirable) characteristics. It should be remembered in this context that people become quite fond of and attached to their pets and that personal reminiscences and expositions on pet African greys are usually contaminated by intense loyalties (and exaggerations). Much of such reporting, it may be mentioned, can best be ascribed to poetic license. The reader will also find, as has been discussed in the main body of the text, that there appears to be no neutral ground concerning the African grey as a desirable pet: either people swear they are the best of parrots or they totally disdain them.

A portion of the text relates to the breeding cycle of the species. It is this body of information which lacks detail and substance. Unfortunately, while the species will breed in captivity if provided the opportunity and appropriate environment—and such breedings are not rare at all—there is little detailed information, even though hours of research were expended to uncover any data which would be a reliable source of assistance to the breeder. While such information is sparse, whatever was available has been itemized in the belief that some information is better than none.

On a personal note, it is hoped that the reader who is seriously embarking on establishing a breeding program for the species will take extra pains to keep detailed notes on his observations and experimentations relating to such breedings. Breeders are encouraged to publish such data, even when utter failure marks the breeding program. Such information is vital, for as noted above there is still much to unravel concerning the species's breeding cycle, particularly those variables which encourage breeding in captivity.

Finally, the conclusion of the text elaborates on the three subspecies of the African grey. Physical descriptions, geographic distributions and the characteristics of each subspecies as a cage bird are given consideration. The reader will note that there is some question concerning one of the subspecies, *Psittacus erithacus princeps* and its status as such. The uncertainty concerning its status is shrouded by historical controversy and by deviations of physical appearance, deviations which are not subspecific per se but which appear to be a general pattern within the species as a whole. Indeed, should *P. e. princeps* actually be a true subspecies, it may very well be that other varieties will have to be recognized as such and categorized, particularly local populations of African greys in the eastern regions of Africa. Whatever the case, I have serious reservations concerning the validity of the subspecific status of *P. e. princeps*. Historical materials are provided presenting both points of view. The reader is encouraged, in the final analysis, to make his own judgment concerning this problem.

Finally, there are two anatonomical illustrations describing the physical topography of a bird and the physical topography of the wing. The reader is encouraged to become familiar with the terms identifying the various regions of the bird's body. While there has been an effort to keep nomenclature to a minimum, complete avoidance was impossible. The reader may find the nomenclature in the illustrations useful in better understanding the passages where such terms are employed.

P. e. erithacus is the most common of the African grey subspecies to be found as a caged bird.

Opposite:
African greys are generally timid and retiring birds. These two specimens of *P. e. timneh* went to the farthest corner of their cage and made every effort to keep a tree trunk (placed in the center of their cage) between them and the photographer.

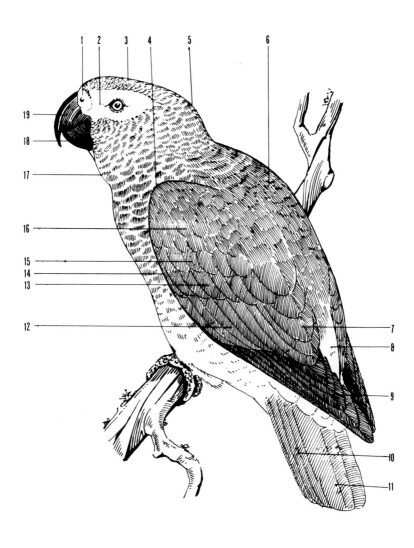

Topography of a parrot: *1*, cere; *2*, lores; *3*, crown; *4*, bend of wing; *5*, nape; *6*, mantle; *7*, tertials; *8*, rump; *9*, primaries; *10*, lateral tail feathers; *11*, central tail feathers; *12*, secondaries; *13*, greater wing coverts; *14*, carpal edge of the wing; *15*, median wing coverts; *16*, lesser wing coverts; *17*, throat; *18*, lower mandible; *19*, upper mandible.

General Characteristics
of the African Grey Parrot

"If a man has ever seen a parrot, it is probably a Grey that he has seen."

— —Dutton

Subspecies and their common names

Psittacus erithacus erithacus Linné: African grey, Grey, Jaco, King Parrot (British, now obsolete)

P. e. timneh Fraser: Timneh

P. e. princeps Boyd Alexander: Princeps, African grey, Grey

Physical size range of *P. erithacus*

Wing: males, 206-260mm; females, 203-255mm
Tail: males, 75-114mm; females, 76-105mm
Culmen: males, 31-39mm; females, 30-40mm
Tarsus: males, 22-28mm; females, 23-28mm

For specific anatomical dimensions for each of the subspecies, refer to the appropriate chapter. *P. e. timneh* is significantly smaller than the other two subspecies; therefore the size dimensions listed above must be viewed with caution, for they are intended only for the purpose of providing the student with a foundation for comparative purposes. Additionally, field studies have shown that there is a cline from west to east, with eastern African greys larger and heavier than comparative populations of the same race in the west of Africa.

Sex Differences: None

As with many other species of birds, the male is generally larger than the female. However, there are males within each race which are smaller than females; size should therefore not be used as a sexing criteria. There is a belief in some quarters that the female's eye is more elliptical than the male's and that the female's "face" is whiter. These opinions have not been substantiated.

Color Characteristics

Psittacus erithacus comprises three races classified as subspecies, two of which are similar enough that there is some doubt concerning one of them, *P. e. princeps*. On the other hand, *P. e. timneh* is so distinct in its coloring and size that some consider it a separate species in itself.

Regardless of distinctions and ornithological debate on the validity of the classification, *Psittacus erithacus* conveys two very distinct impressions. The first impression is that the parrot has about it a demeanor of wisdom and intelligence. This impression is no doubt encouraged by the species's uncanny ability to imitate a particular human voice one moment and then a few seconds later mimic another voice in a completely different intonation, dialect, pitch and quality. Its mimicry is the most human-like of all the parrots. Further, conditioned verbal reflexes can be easily established in the individual bird so that its guise of wisdom and intelligence is enhanced by its ability to respond with seemingly appropriate phrases to appropriate stimuli.

The second impression one gets is that the African grey is a shy and retiring bird, rarely appearing to willingly accept human friendship and companionship. It is the rare specimen which becomes a pet, although most are easily tamed and trained. At best most African greys, once tamed, can be said to tolerate people. Similarly, however, while few African greys can be said to become pets in the traditional sense of the word, even fewer prove irascible or aggressive. If anything, the species has a personality which is relatively flat, one which lacks the vivacity common to most other parrots.

Because of these contradictory impressions, there are diverse reactions to the African grey. Because of the species's international reputation as an unexcelled talker and because of the illusion of wisdom and intelligence which the species conveys, some consider the African grey the ultimate talking parrot. Others, however, find *Psittacus erithacus* unattractive and undesirable for a variety of reasons. There is considerable objection to the species's lack of "personality," a factor which some aviculturists feel results in a tamed African grey sitting for hours on end on the highest point of its cage without so much as one sound or movement. Because of this particular personality quirk and the species's somewhat squat appearance, the African grey unfortunately has the appearance of a vulture for many. Others object to the species's simplicity of appearance and its lack of flamboyant colors. It is often described as drab. Yet there are those who find the grey coloration unique, having considerable esthetic appeal.

Since values are relative, it is really not possible to define the species in esthetic and behavioral terms in a manner that would be agreeable to all. There is, however, universal agreement that *Psittacus erithacus* has an excellent reputation for its talking ability and that that reputation is well deserved.

Head Coloration: While most of the head is a pastel, soft-toned gray, the facial area is a (more or less) grayish white coloration. The two colors are so distinct that from a distance the facial region almost appears white. Beginning with the lower forehead adjacent to the upper mandible and cere, the grayish white coloration extends backward toward and including the lores and midpoint ear-coverts. This lighter coloration does not include the crown, throat, nape or chin. The entire width of the grayish white coloration at its widest point is from the cere to the lower edge of the upper mandible.

All other parts of the head are a tone of gray which can be described as soft and pleasant. This shading remains true in tone and hue with breast feathers, but the gray of the crown and lower nape plumage gradually intensifies into a darker shade similar to the back covering. The differences in tone, however, are slight.

The beak is an ebony black with a medium gloss to it. A small area of the upper mandible, including the cere, is a grayish white. The beak is less severe and prominent as compared to those in the genus *Amazona*, although its curve is heavier.

The iris is a lemon tone, while the cere itself is whitish.

Wings: The upper wing-coverts are a deeper and duskier gray than the breast and head regions. There is little variation in the overall coloration of the various wing feathers except for the primaries which are black and the under wing-coverts which are a slightly lighter shade of gray.

Body: The breast feathers, like the head feathers, are a soft pastel gray with the tone and hue remaining consistent except for the lower abdominal and rump areas. These areas are a much lighter tone, a more whitish gray shade. The breast feathers have a scalloped appearance due to the barely perceptible tinge of white on their terminal margins. The back feathers are intermediate in tone between the grays of the breast and wing plumage.

Tail: The under tail-coverts are, depending on the race, a bright red, maroon-brown or gray. The tail feathers are, also depending on race, either bright vermilion, maroon-brown or gray.

Feet: The inner thighs are a slightly lighter shade than the outer thigh feathers. The feet are black, but they appear as if the bird had just walked through a sack of flour.

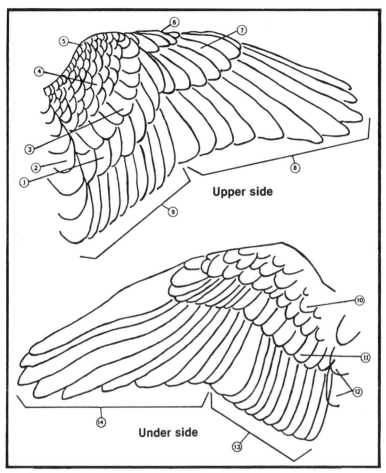

Parts of a Wing

1, Secondary coverts; *2*, Tertials; *3*, Median wing coverts; *4*, Lesser wing coverts; *5*, Bend of wing; *6*, Carpal edge; *7*, Primary coverts; *8*, Primaries; *9*, Secondaries; *10*, Lesser under wing coverts; *11*, Greater under wing coverts; *12*, Axillaries; *13*, Secondaries; *14*, Primaries.

Immatures: Immature birds have extremely dark gray irises, almost black. The under tail-coverts are generally predominantly gray rather than red, maroon-brown or pink-tinged.

Geographic Distribution of the Species

Psittacus erithacus enjoys an extensive range which covers the greater equatorial part of Africa from west to east. Its range is almost exclusively restricted to the great rain forests which stretch as a belt across the continent.

Its range extends from Guinea in the west to the western provinces of Kenya and Tanzania in the east. Its most northerly reach seems to be the Ubangi River, which forms the boundary between Zaire and the Central African Empire. To the south the species is found in the south-central regions of Zaire, extending westward throughout the country to northern Angola on the Atlantic coast. Its territorial range along the Atlantic coast includes all of the countries north of Angola bordering the Gulf of Guinea. There is some question concerning the actual most easterly extent of the species's range. This problem is discussed later.

Based on published materials and the total range of the species as currently understood, the areas in which *Psittacus erithacus* may be found are as follows:

Locales in which the species has been reported: Guinea, Liberia, Sierra Leone, Ivory Coast, Ghana, Nigeria, Congo, Angola, Zaire, Tanzania, Uganda, Kenya, Togo, Cameroon, and the islands of Principé and São Tomé.

Locales which fall within the territorial range of the species but about which there are no published records: Central African Republic, Rwanda, Burundi, Equatorial Guinea, and Gabon.

Locales close to international boundaries which may have some small isolated populations: northwestern Zambia, southeastern Sudan, Lake Rudolph region of Ethiopia, southwestern Upper Volta, and southeastern Mali.

Behavior in the Wild

Most early accounts of European exploratory expeditions into equatorial Africa during the previous century never fail to mention the great numbers of African greys observed

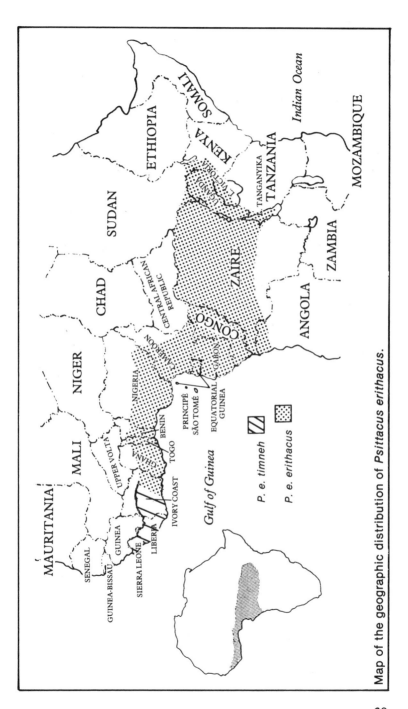

Map of the geographic distribution of *Psittacus erithacus*.

P. e. timneh

P. e. erithacus

throughout most localities traversed and charted. Sir Henry Morton Stanley made reference to them in his journals. Stanley was the famous nineteenth-century English explorer who spent much of his life exploring Africa. His work resulted in significant contributions being made to the understanding of the geographic and natural character of the "Dark Continent." (Some of his observations were included by W.T. Greene in *Parrots in Captivity,* 1887.)

It was, however, J.G. Keulemans, a prominent ornithologist and naturalist during the second half of the previous century, who exhaustively recorded his observations of the species. Keulemans, also an adventurer and painter, spent considerable time in Africa between 1880 (?) and 1886 (?). (As with Stanley and others, W.T. Greene quoted extensively from one of Keulemans's original works.) He seemed awed by the parrot, noting that "on Princeps Island we find these birds [*i.e., princeps*] in great abundance . . . nowhere on the continent of Africa are these birds so plentiful." At one point, as he relates an experience in which he and his party concealed themselves to more closely study (and capture) the greys, he said that "at this time we must have been surrounded by hundreds of Parrots."

Keulemans's estimates about the number could have been colored, of course, by his excitement on observing at firsthand parrots which were commonly known throughout Europe, which were popular and which at that time were credited with great wisdom and intelligence. For some years afterwards, subsequent expeditions were to continue to confirm his observations of large flocks. Around the turn of the century, however, reports appearing in ornithological publications noted the species's apparent decrease in numbers since Keulemans's original studies. Perhaps it is the interpretation of Keulemans's report which influenced later conclusions drawn by subsequent explorers, adventurers and scientists and led them to believe that the species had significantly decreased in numbers. An excellent example of interpretation biasing a finding can be seen in the opinion of Boyd Alexander, an experienced naturalist and ornithologist. In a letter published in *The Ibis* (1900), Alexander summarized his comments about the African grey by concluding: "The Parrot appears to be decreasing very much. Keulemans in his day (1867) reckoned them by the thousands, but at the present time they could hardly be told by the hundred."

It is important to note that nowhere in his writings does Keulemans estimate the greys in one sighting as numbering in the thousands; he refers to them as "hundreds," and even such an estimate must be held suspect because it is nebulous. Nevertheless, numerous other reports conclude by commenting on the decrease in numbers. Marchant, for example, wrote in 1942, that *Psittacus erithacus* was "widespread in the forest belt, but nowhere common." In fact, because of the popularity of the African grey as a pet, it was generally believed by field expeditions that the decrease in the population was due to overharvesting of the species. At least one ornithologist (Lowe, 1937) was to write: "It is hoped, now that the market for live birds is closed, that they will increase in numbers."

While some of these field expedition reports present a bleak account of the African grey's population profile, the exact status of the species's numbers over its widespread territory is not exactly clear. There are numerous other reports which strongly suggest that the species is anything but suffering a sharp decrease in population. For example, scarcely two years after Lowe's note that the ban on importation would give the species a respite and an opportunity to replenish its ranks, Chapin (1939) was to write this:

> Near Lukolela I watched them come to sleep on a group of a half-dozen Borassus palms in a grassy area surrounded by forest, until the assemblage numbered approximately two hundred. The stur-

dy leaves of the palms were already bowed down permanently from the parrots' weight.

Chapin's account of the species numbers is by no means alone. There are several others. For example, in 1950 Snow was to report that they were "abundant," and in 1965 Serle reported seeing several hundred in a silk-cotton tree.

These conclusions are based, of course, on comparisons between the various estimates reported from the field. But the estimates resulting from field work are dependent on a number of variables. If a comparison is made with the kind of estimate Keulemans made, then a serious and erroneous conclusion could be drawn, for "hundreds" can mean a different amount to different people. Also, expeditions could be made into terrains in which (for some reason or another) there were no significant numbers of the species available for observation on that particular occasion. For example, Charles C. Young wrote in 1946 that he had seen several flocks during mornings and evenings, but "between December and February they are much less in evidence." One field worker may be more conservative or more liberal in his estimates than another.

While the species is still generally considered widespread and common throughout its range, it is, however, no longer considered common near towns and villages (Forshaw, 1977). Part of this decrease in numbers near populated areas can be attributed to a variety of factors. In the first place, as will shortly be discussed more thoroughly, *Psittacus erithacus* is a shy and retiring bird. "They are very suspicious, and always on the alert, taking notice of everything that comes in their vicinity" (Greene, 1887). They consequently seek refuge during feeding and resting in only the tallest of nearby trees. As mature trees are felled for industrial and agricultural purposes near populated areas, the species is forced to seek forested regions relatively unscathed by the lumberman's ax. In addition, as Bannerman reported in 1912, and as has been subsequently concluded by other students of ornithology, the absence of *Psittacus erithacus* near villages and towns is not just a matter of competition between cocoa plantations and the species, but also is a result of the fact that the "planters shoot a good many for food."

Even given this pressure around agriculturally developed areas, the species has become by no means scarce. With increased acreage being converted to maize crops, it may be that the species is changing its foraging habits, thereby adapting to the environmental change. It has in fact been reported (Mackworth-Praed and Grant, 1952) that African greys now do extensive damage to maize crops and "have become so bold as to be driven away only with great difficulty." Sharpe reported the following in 1907:

> The common Grey Parrot is fond of maize and the flocks gather about the patches of corn while it is still ripe. It is the work of the girls of the village to scare the Parrot away. The girls keep up a noise all day long, by drumming on logs, while the Parrots hang around persistently, watching for a chance to get a bite, yet afraid of the noise. When they get the opportunity, they gorge themselves. A Grey Parrot has been caught alive from sheer inability to fly readily, owing to the weight of grain in its crop.

Sharpe's report is by no means atypical. Damage to crops is extensive and now reportedly common.

Aside from agricultural or nuisance reasons, another prime reason for the reduction of the numbers of African greys near settled areas is their commercial value in the pet trade. Their popularity as pets both in Africa and beyond is legend, and it should therefore not be surprising that African landowners jealously guard any trees on their land that may have nesting greys in them so that the fledglings can be taken for the pet trade.

In short, while it is clear that their numbers are decreasing near well-populated areas, whether or not they are decreasing in number in less populated areas is not as definite. Given its shyness, it probably is holding its own. As van Someren (1916) concludes, "They are difficult to obtain, for they fly high and swiftly." As a matter of fact, *Psittacus erithacus* may be adapting to human encroachment through another means of avoidance, for it appears to be extending its range throughout equatorial Africa (Mackworth-Praed and Grant, 1952).

Among themselves African greys are highly gregarious birds, preferring to be in the company of their fellows. While there are occasional reports of solitary birds or solitary pairs (Bannerman, 1953), such accounts are the exception to the rule and are generally found in those field reports noting a general scarcity of the species in a given locality. Most field observations report the species in flocks of twenty or so individuals and, as we have seen, sometimes in flocks several times larger. This gregariousness even extends to nesting practices in which "many nests are found within a few feet of each other, and often in one tree, two or more holes may be seen occupied by hatching pairs" (Greene, 1887).

Seeking out the tallest trees in a forested region, the grey prefers to remain, if possible, at the edge of the forest. If there is a lake or stream nearby with a forested island on it, the African grey will roost there. The species will continue using the same roosting site until food supplies dwindle with the changing seasons and the birds are required to find new feeding grounds. There is a strong relationship between feeding and roosting sites, for the species's feeding habits directly depend on the particular fruits and seeds that may be in season at a particular time. When the fruits are no longer available, the species is forced to locate a different seasonal food supply, and its roosting site may consequently be changed. Until the site is discarded as a result of necessity, the species will continue using that site faithfully from night to night.

The flight to the roosting site each evening is accompanied by considerable "shrill whistles when on the wing" (van Someren, 1916) and punctuated with "loud cries" (Bannerman, 1953). "As sunset draws on, the Parrots may be seen in parties winging their way . . . and on reaching it [the roosting site] take their places in the trees" (Greene, 1878). Their screeches are usually harsh and unpleasant but the harshness is frequently "interrupted by clear, pleasant whistles" (Chapin, 1939). Greene (1878) quotes an unidentified writer who described the greys during flight: "Flocks of Grey Parrots flew across the sky, alternatively screeching and whistling melodiously."

Various writers have commented on the grey's diurnal habits. "For a truly diurnal bird the grey parrot is exceptional in its habit of flying about and calling well after night has begun to fall" (Chapin, 1939). Even when dark has fallen, pairs of African greys continue winging in to the roosting site. Well into the night, as Keulemans reported, "a few sounds may be heard at intervals which most probably proceed from some belated bird seeking a place or a quarrel: sometimes in the dead of the night the whole colony is thrown into an uproar" (Greene, 1878).

With the sunrise, even before the early rays of the sun begin to break the horizon, the parrots leave their roosting tree in twos and threes and make way to their feeding grounds (Serle, 1965). As at all other times, their flight is well above the treetops; this flight is again accompanied by considerable screeching and whistling. The flight is sure and swift and the wing beat is shallow and rapid, more like that of a duck, "the red tail and under tail-coverts . . . noticeable" (Bannerman, 1953). Within a few minutes the entire roosting site has been abandoned, and the flock is at the feeding grounds feeding on whatever fruits are then in season.

The diet of *Psittacus erithacus* consists primarily of fruits and various seeds, preferring the seeds "rather soft and green" (Chapin, 1939). The palm nut, however, is preferred above all else. Showing a high degree of adaptability, the species has also shown a preference for maize even when there may be an adequate supply of their traditional foods available. They are rarely seen on the ground searching for food or engaged otherwise in diverse pursuits; but judging from the fact that Chapin (1939) found quartz in the stomachs of some dissected African greys, it appears that at times they do come to the ground to feed.

Depending on the food supplies available during a particular season, *Psittacus erithacus* prefers to feed in lowland forests, although they do visit and feed in open country and savanna (Forshaw, 1977). When feeding in tall trees, however, "these parrots . . . might escape notice were it not for their raucous voices" (Chapin, 1939). During feeding at the very tips of the trees, they climb from branch to branch, unlike most other species of birds which will hop or fly from one branch to another in pursuit of choice morsels.

It is interesting to note that most pet owners and aviculturists feed their captive African greys a diet which is almost always solely comprised of peanuts, sunflower seeds and safflower seeds, an abominable departure from the species's more balanced diet in the wild.

Breeding and Nesting Behavior

Number of Eggs

Most of the scientific and avicultural articles report that the "normal" number of eggs per nest is two and on occasion three. This view is so common that there is no need to identify all of the numerous sources reporting this clutch size.

A detailed study of the available literature which is based on sightings where the eggs were *actually* counted suggests, however, that the "normal clutch of two" is more an *inaccurate generalization than an established fact.* I identified twenty-six references pertaining to observed clutches of captive birds; the evidence strongly suggests that in at least sixty percent of all clutches, the average clutch has three or four eggs, and that four eggs can be expected at least twenty-five percent of the time. There are no reports of five eggs and only two reports of two eggs per clutch.

Another interesting and very important variable related to egg laying by *Psittacus erithacus* concerns individual hens which have laid successive clutches. The number of eggs laid by a hen on one occasion is generally the number of eggs she can be expected to lay in future clutches.

The following paragraphs detail the reported clutches of African greys in captivity. While the figures speak for themselves, the reader must be careful in the final interpretation of this sparse data. Dates are given whenever they were reported, but some reports only gave dates of the chicks' first sounds being heard. The month of egg laying is my approximation based on the information reported by the breeder. It is dangerous to draw absolute conclusions from these few cases. However, as the statisticians express it, "the data suggest a trend." It is hoped that future study will clarify this issue.

• Mrs. Wright ("Editorial Note," *Aviculture*, 1945): The same hen had four different nests. The number of eggs per nest was unreported, but there were twelve surviving chicks. The date the eggs were laid was not reported.

• Walter Landberg (1958): The same hen had four different clutches. The first clutch of four eggs, laid June 16-27, was infertile. The second clutch, laid August 4-16, had four eggs. The third clutch, laid June 17-26, had four eggs. The fourth clutch had four eggs, but the date the eggs were laid is unknown. There were twelve surviving chicks.

• Mickey Hensel (1978): One clutch of four eggs was laid, possibly in October. All chicks survived.

• Gilbert Lee (1938-39): The first hen had four clutches. The first clutch, laid August 17, had three eggs; one hatched but died shortly after. The second clutch, laid November 15, had three eggs; all chicks hatched, but one died. The third clutch, laid April 12, had four eggs; all chicks survived. The fourth clutch, laid August 29, had four eggs; all chicks survived. The second hen's first clutch, laid October 4, had four eggs; all chicks survived. The second clutch, laid December 6-11, had three eggs; all chicks survived.

• Reid (Seth-Smith, 1939): Three eggs were laid August 6-13. All chicks hatched, but only two survived.

• Tavistock (1929): One hen laid two clutches of four eggs each; the egg laying dates are unknown. All of the eggs were infertile; there was no cock.

• Clifford Smith (1968): The first hen had three clutches. The first clutch had one egg which might have been laid in June; the one chick survived. The second clutch of two eggs was laid July 16-30; both chicks survived. The third clutch of three eggs, possibly laid in July, had two survivors. The second hen had two clutches. Only one chick survived from the first clutch; the exact number of

A trio of one-month-old African grey chicks.

eggs laid, possibly in June, is unknown. The second clutch of two eggs might have been laid in May or June; both chicks survived.

• Eve Wicks (1964): One chick survived from a clutch of three eggs which were possibly laid in July or August.

• Edward Boosey (1945): The first clutch, possibly laid in April, contained an unknown number of eggs; one chick survived. An unknown number of eggs were laid in the second clutch; one nestling survived (at the time of reporting). The date the second clutch was laid is unknown.

• U.G. Lister (1962): The same hen had two clutches. The first clutch, laid January 2, had one egg; it hatched but was killed by the parent. The second clutch, laid December 6-11, had three eggs; all chicks survived.

• K.W. Dalton (1957): The same hen had two clutches. The first clutch, possibly laid in May, had four eggs; all eggs were infertile. The second clutch, possibly laid in June, had four eggs; three eggs hatched and two chicks survived.

• "A Floridian" ("The Nest Box," *Aviculture*, 1943): Two chicks survived from one clutch; the date of egg laying and the number of eggs laid are unknown.

Size and Color of Eggs

The eggs are pure white, partially glossy and ovate. There appears to be considerable variation in egg size, but as has been noted from field studies in Africa, the sizes of the birds themselves are not uniform from one end of their range to the other: there is a general cline toward larger birds the more eastward the population. This cline in size could account for the considerable variation of egg size, which is now considered as 31.5-39.7mm × 29-38.5mm. Mackworth-Praed and Grant (1952) report egg sizes of 31-39mm × 33-45mm from clutches in the Lake Victoria region, the species's most easterly habitat; this size is considerably larger than the former.

Breeding Behavior in the Wild

Field observations of *Psittacus erithacus* reveals no fixed seasonal breeding period, except that the species may nest any time from August to January. This six- to seven-month differential occurs because the birds breed during different months depending on the region which they inhabit. In Uganda, for example, Mackworth-Praed and Grant (1952) reported that the species breeds between July and September. Chapin observed during his field studies in 1939 that the parrots appeared to breed during the rainy seasons, and he found a nesting pair on December 12 (whether the pair were sitting on the eggs, brooding them or caring for nestlings is not clear) at Lukolela. Earlier, in the northern region of Ituri at Medje, he had found nests during both August and September (again, the stage of development of the offspring is not clear). He also reported that he saw nestlings being offered for sale during February. Serle (1957), on the other hand, observed that the birds in the Niger Delta bred during the dry season. During January he was taken to a tree in which a clutch of eggs being incubated was found. That same day, interestingly enough, Serle was shown several nestlings in different stages of development being offered for sale by local Africans to the pet trade.

Judging from other information which comes from breeders who have successfully bred the species in northern countries such as Britain, it appears that the species also has a very flexible breeding schedule in captivity.

In the wild the species chooses towering trees for its nesting sites. Serle (1957) reported finding a nest one hundred feet above the ground, Chapin (1939) a nest seventy-five feet above the ground and Bannerman (1953) succinctly describes nests found only in the "highest trees." As with all other variables related to the life of *Psittacus erithacus*, the species prefers to remain aloof and distant during nesting and finds absolute seclusion only in the haven of towering trees. The seclusion is complete, for, as Serle (1957) wryly notes, "the nests are inaccessible to all but a skilled rope climber."

Because of the nests' inaccessibility and the difficulty in climbing to them, there is little field information available about the nest itself, or about sitting, brooding, feeding and growth patterns. What reports there are are scanty at best and meager in the insight they provide. Bannerman (1953) described a nesting site simply as a "hole in the trunk." Chapin (1939) made note of a knot hole in an isolated tree which a pair of greys were seen to enter from time to time; a native climber was induced to climb the tree, but all that was reported was that there were eggs in the nest. The only detailed report, if it can be called that, is by Serle (1957), who observed that the nest which was examined had a clutch of three eggs which were sitting on a layer of sawdust and debris at the bottom of a two-foot hole in the tree. Little else is reported.

Breeding in Captivity

While it is generally believed that *Psittacus erithacus* is difficult to breed in captivity, the reports published in various journals over the previous century would suggest otherwise. The literature shows that successful breedings have taken place on quite a number of occasions in such diverse countries as Nigeria, Great Britain, Germany, the United States (both southern and northern regions) and others. As a matter of fact, there has been such success in the breeding of greys that one American breeder, Gilbert Lee, ran several successive advertisements over several years during the Depression; advertisements of 1935 included: "We Breed Them Here in Los Angeles"; "Discount to Wholesalers—lots of three or more"; and "Think of it, you can order a baby African Grey Parrot. We fill the order by breeding them here in Los Angeles . . . guaranteed to live and talk . . . $125.00 each, terms to suit your pocketbook." It should be emphasized that these advertisements occurred over several years and were not the result of optimistic daydreaming!

After reading the literature, one suspects, however, that such a mythology has developed about the so-called unbreedability of the species in captivity that the myth is accepted as the gospel truth and there are consequently few attempts by aviculturists to pursue the issue further. When such breedings do occur, the event is considered such a miracle that the breeder in question zealously pursues the recognition which is awarded breeders of so-called difficult-to-breed species.

This mythology or belief can best be illustrated by some of Edward Boosey's comments made in 1945, after he had been the first British breeder to be officially recognized for breeding the greys. Boosey was an avid and successful British aviculturist and, it might be noted, was highly competent in avicultural science, for he was also the first to successfully breed the blue-fronted Amazon *(Amazona aestiva)* in captivity in Great Britain. He expressed the view that the lack of successful breeding in Britain was in good measure related to the public's perception of the species. In

A pair of African greys used this hollowed-out log, placed high in the aviary, for a nest site.

part, the public viewed the African grey as a pet which should be put in a cage and taught to talk. He illustrated his point with an anecdote about visitors who when shown a baby African grey which was born in captivity in Britain would invariably exclaim what Boosey calls the "inevitable remark": "But I didn't know they could be bred!"

In reviewing the literature, however, one soon realizes that the breeding of the African grey is by no means a random and miraculous event. Some breeders such as Gilbert Lee and Walther Landberg have repeatedly demonstrated that not only can they achieve success with one pair a successive number of times, but that they can also be successful with several pairs.

Yet skepticism abounds; this matter will be further explored shortly, for it undoubtedly contributes to the lack of effort to breed *Psittacus erithacus*. In spite of this skepticism, there have been some concentrated efforts to breed greys, and sometimes, as in the following history, the methodology would be considered novel, bizarre and even impossible by conventional and orthodox aviculturists.

Gilbert Lee first began breeding the species in 1903 when as a young man of twenty or so he encountered his first African grey in New York City, was impressed with its retail price at the time and saw an excellent economic opportunity. The uniqueness of his experiment is worth quoting in detail from the original 1930 text:

> I purchased seventeen [African grey parrots, subspecies unidentified] and placed them in a loft in a friend's cow barn in [New] Jersey. Three years later sixty-seven birds had been added to the original number placed in this loft and eleven skeletons were found. The birds never saw a human being after being placed in the loft, consequently no pictures were taken.
>
> The entire loft was lined with ¾ inch wire netting to keep out the rats and to allow climbing around. There was a continuous water supply regulated so that two or three porcelain dishes were kept filled, and the attendant saw to it that there was a slight overflow from these raised dishes to keep the four or five inches of sawdust that was scattered over the damp floor wet and cause some rotting.
>
> The nests were hung from the ceiling on hay wire wrapped around some small branches; some were barrels cut in half, partially filled with peat moss and sawdust; others were rotten logs hung vertically, and some horizontally. Soap boxes were also nailed to the wall, all the same "pigeon style." All the entrances to the nests, and in fact many of the nests, were covered with Florida moss, hay, etc., in order to give the birds more

seclusion. Ordinary chicken hoppers were used, which had a connection from the outside to put in hemp, sunflower, millet, canary and clover-grass seed. The sawdust on the floor being damp, much of the wasted seed sprouted and was readily eaten by both young and old alike.

In one end of the loft was a half-inch hardware square-netting basket and under it a box of bran. Occasionally, a calf's head was thrown in and while I never saw the parrots eat any of the fresh or decayed meat, nevertheless they relished the maggots which dropped from the basket.

This loft being in a dairy barn made it convenient occasionally to slip in by way of the trap door pans of sour milk or cottage cheese. I put in a chute, the entrance of which was on the outside, which went down to the centre of the room. Mixed feed was thrown daily down this chute.

One can readily imagine the amount of skepticism that Lee must have encountered as a result of his disclosure of this rather extraordinary breeding program. Indeed, his experiment was conducted when puritanical Victorianism still controlled traditional and unresilient standards and beliefs, and aviculturists must have been appalled by his methods and suspicious of his results. His work was conducted, it must be remembered, in an age when pairs of birds were considered married and hens were referred to as wives, cocks as husbands and so on. It was also only after a great deal of persuasion that Lee wrote an article about that experiment.

Over thirty years later when Lee had begun breeding greys again, but in a more orthodox and aviculturally acceptable way, he (1938-39) wrote: "Some believed the story of raising them in a flock in a cow barn loft, while others did not, and they gave good reasons why this writer was a person to be doubted and exposed." Judging from Mr. Lee's choice of the word "exposed," it can be left to the reader's imagination the kinds of accusations which must have been hurled at Lee and his work!

The fact that Lee himself admits to the skepticism of others may not assure the contemporary reader that Lee had indeed been successful and that his experiment was not a figment of his imagination, a horrid figment by avicultural standards. The fact is that when the price of African greys approached $100 or so per specimen during the 1930's because the quarantine was instituted in the United States, Mr. Lee resumed his breeding efforts, but this time in a more conventional manner. He not only was successful once, but he also repeated this success innumerable times. After his death in 1941, his work was carried on just as successfully by his wife. He was successful, it should also be noted, at a time when few others could speak of successfully breeding the grey. In the forthcoming pages more will be mentioned about Mr. Lee's success and the methods he employed.

Another example of what was considered an unorthodox breeding program was cited by Edward Boosey in a somewhat scornful and contemptuous tone in an article published in *Avicultural Magazine* in 1945. Mr. Boosey had been successful in breeding a pair of greys and successful in rearing the surviving youngster into adulthood. His success was considered extraordinary, at least as far as Mr. Boosey was concerned. He evidently convinced the British Avicultural Society that it was extraordinary, as later he received the society's medal for the breeding—because there were no official written records of previous successful breedings in England. Boosey went to a considerable length to review the history of previous reported successful breedings, which he promptly discounted as being of no importance for one reason or another. In discussing one such instance, one which would have been perfectly acceptable at the time it took place during the early nineteenth century but which would have seemed preposterous to Mr. Boosey and his colleagues, he wrote:

> I gather that the only known record of Greys bred here in confinement comes from Yorkshire, where some are reputed to have been hatched and reared—of all improbable places—in a copper with a 'nest of flannel' in the bottom, placed near (thank goodness not over) a fire.
>
> As, however, this account is rather more than a hundred years old and third hand in the bargain, I doubt whether much importance could be attached to it.

It appears, however, that there was considerable rivalry—and perhaps jealousy involving anyone's possible successful breeding of *Psittacus erithacus,* which always has and still does enjoy considerable prestige and popularity as a pet. Perhaps that accounts for the fact that aside from a very, very few exceptions, almost every article publishing the results of a successful breeding of greys provides nothing but the briefest, most peripheral and nebulous details about how this event was encouraged to take place.

This rivalry seemed to be quite intense, without any admission that there was indeed a serious effort to gather all the honors while at the same time discrediting others. In retrospect it all seems so very foolish—but understandable, considering that the African grey has been held in such high esteem yet considered so unbreedable in captivity, at least as popular opinion would have it.

Edward Boosey again involved himself in a public controversy in 1952-53. In the May-June issue of *Avicultural Magazine,* he virtually challenged a contemporary aviculturist in India who had contended that breedings of the African grey on the subcontinent of India were so successful that breeders "hardly knew what to do with the young ones." Boosey's opposition appears to have stemmed from his inability to believe that anyone could provide conditions which greys would find suitable for mating and the rearing of young, in quantity at that. His arrogance in the matter led to an exchange of letters. He finally wrote a concealed apology, which was published in the July-August issue of the magazine.

It is interesting to note that Boosey's attitude toward the breeding of African greys by other breeders was somewhat akin to the attitude which greeted Lee's success in the United States after he announced the results of his barn loft experiment. It must be remembered, however, that because of the seeming unbreedability of the grey, any successful mating results were bound to achieve considerable fame and reputation for the breeder involved. In the context of what seemed to be a sole achievement, is understandable for a breeder to toot his own horn so to speak. Boosey (1950) even went so far as to claim that his successful breeding and the rearing of the young "was the first young parrot ever to be bred in confinement in this country, or, I believe in Europe."

While it is easy in retrospect to apply labels and criticism, in all fairness Mr. Boosey cannot really be faulted for responding the way he did. As an avid aviculturist, whose work over the following years would earn him recognition for breeding two parrots and the British avicultural community's highest esteem, he simply reflected the stereotypes and values of his time.

There had, however, been successes prior to Mr. Boosey's achievement. As Dr. W.T. Greene notes in *Parrots in Captivity*, Buffon relates that in his time a pair of these birds bred for several years consecutively in Paris, and reared their young; this statement, however, has been questioned by some more recent writers, but it is, nevertheless, probably quite correct, for a pair belonging to the late Mr. Charles Buxton, M.P., made a nest in a hollow branch and "brought up two young Grey parrots, which were afflicted with the most awful tempers. The party of four fly about almost always together, and are a great ornament to the place." Given Dr. Greene's reputation both as a bird fancier, aviculturist and authority in the field, it is doubtful that he would misrepresent the facts, or indeed that the Member of Parliament would distort them, particularly before an association of (skeptical) ornithologists and aviculturists! Suffice it to say that the species will breed in captivity if given the opportunity to follow its instincts and drives, and such breedings are anything but rare and random events.

Mating Behavior

There are, nevertheless, some fundamental problems related to the successful breeding of *Psittacus erithacus*. Because it is difficult to accurately and unfailingly distinguish males from females (although males tend to be slightly larger on the average), birds of the same sex are frequently put into the same aviary together. (This is not a problem unique to the greys, for there are numerous species of birds in which there is little or no difference between the sexes.) Sometimes, therefore, it may take a third or fourth grey introduced into the flight before a pairing will result. The problem is somewhat compounded, however, by what seems to be a preponderance of females exported from Africa and a minimum of males, at least, according to various breeders.

Clifford Smith suffered from this problem before he was able to embark on a successful breeding program. After successfully breeding one pair, he decided he would obtain another pair from a bird fancier-dealer who assured him that "they were a pair." He wrote in 1968: "When I bought a similar bird from the same fancier-dealer, also claimed to be a cock, I did not hesitate to put all three together. Within a few days the latest bird was feeding the bird sold to me as a cock of the pair." Of course, the original birds were both females, but there was no way of knowing this at the time.

Generally, when mature greys of opposite sexes are introduced to each other, the male begins feeding the female. This, of course, is a strong indication that the pair are interested in mating and setting up a nest. Courting behavior also includes considerable mutual head scratching and beak rubbing. In short, while there may initially be an absence of copulatory behavior, there is a great deal of mutual affection displayed.

Smith encouraged the development of interest between the male and female by first separating them with a wire mesh. After several days he introduced them into an aviary which had a nest already in it. Smith reported that within five minutes of being introduced into the aviary the pair disappeared into the nest box. Smith's methods seem to work, for he has been successful on several occasions in breeding not only wild but also tame greys.

The nesting place itself seems crucial. If we can recall the earlier discussion of the birds' behavior in the wild, it will be remembered that the species prefers seclusion and distance not only in its nesting activities but also in its everyday activities. It chooses trees which are towering and virtually inaccessible to anything that could be a threat.

Successful breeders have achieved favorable results by presenting the pair with a breeding site which, while considerably different from that which would be chosen by a pair in the wild, at least resembles an adequate nesting site.

The types used vary from breeder to breeder, but the effect is always the same: "A small barrel fixed on its side inside a box" (Seth-Smith, 1939); "A nest box of a 'grandfather-clock type' six feet high by ten by twelve inches" (Smith, 1968); "A one-foot square by four-foot nest box made out of three-quarters-inch wood" (Hensel, 1978).

The bottom of the nesting site is generally covered with

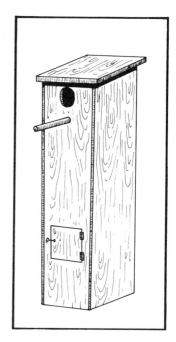

A "grandfather-clock type" nest box. Breeding pairs of African greys have successfully used this type of box for a nest site.

sawdust, wood shavings, peat moss or chopped turfs. When the pair are prepared to nest, the female will throw out various nesting materials as she prepares the nest for her eggs. Usually, too, the hen may cover this nesting material with down plucked from her breast (Seth-Smith, 1939).

Of course it is assumed that a suitable flight has been prepared for the pair. While it may seem trite, a flight which does not meet the minimal living space for a species which displays such needs for seclusion will be inadequate indeed and will discourage any serious efforts by the pair to nest. Smith (1968), for example, provided flights which proved room enough for his pairs; the flights were ten feet long, five feet wide and six feet high.

Given that the species is prone to breed during the latter part of the summer or the early part of autumn in northern climates, the weather may be inclement enough to prove deleterious to the health of the offspring and the success of the brooding pair. The pair should be protected from strong winds and other inclement weather. Where there is a strong possibility that excessive bad weather can affect the young before they fledge (northern countries), outdoor flights usually have the nesting box in a small enclosed shed attached to the flight. This is important when the young chicks are being reared by their parents, for often it will be November and the young will still not have fledged.

Another incentive to successful mating and nesting has been the introduction of various foods and minerals into the flight as soon as it is observed that the pair are taking an active courtship interest in each other. Once a pair began showing such interest, Seth-Smith (1939) ground up cuttlebone, old mortar and considerable lime and sprinkled it over the parrots' food. These kinds of minerals are essential to ensure that the eggs are not laid soft-shelled, a problem faced by Hensel (1978) for two years.

Nesting Behavior

Most parrot hens lay an egg every second day until the clutch is complete. The African grey, however, does not reflect a consistency of this type. The second egg may follow two or three days later. If there is a third or fourth egg, these may be laid as much as five or six days apart. With large clutches, therefore, there may be as much as a two-week difference in the growing chicks, so that there is always the danger than the youngest chick(s) may not get enough food or may be suffocated, particularly if the nesting area is too small. Conversely, if the nesting box is too big, the youngest chick may not be adequately brooded during inclement weather in the autumn; it may be overexposed to the cold. This is not so much a problem as in the first instance of a crowded nest box, for both parents generally brood at night.

During incubation it is the hen which sits on the eggs; she remains constant in her care except during the very early morning and late afternoon when she may leave the nest for brief periods. While it is usually the hen which assumes sitting responsibilities, Dalton (1957) noted that in the successful breeding of his *timneh* and *erithacus* pairs both hen and cock remained in the nest, except during those times needed for feeding. During the hen's sojourn on the eggs, the cock regularly and constantly feeds her at the nesting site. He usually either descends into the nest itself or feeds her at the entrance to the nest. Sometimes, as Smith (1968) observed, the cock may even feed the hen when she is away from the nest.

Once the eggs have hatched, the cock becomes involved in feeding the young chicks. By the end of the first week he is faithfully and regularly attending to the chicks' needs for food (Smith, 1968).

The cock's attendance to the chicks is so intense that it led Boosey (1945) to conclude that the cock had assumed almost all of the responsibility for feeding the offspring. There is no concrete evidence pointing to a consistent pattern which would either support or reject this contention, however.

Brooding is shared by both parents. It continues on a regular basis for at least two months, after which time spent brooding in the nest declines and more time is spent in the flight, as parental interest in the offspring and brooding wanes. But even during the intense initial period, brooding is tempered by climatic conditions. Dalton (1957) observed that when the weather was exceptionally hot, neither parent brooded during the day; and when the weather was damp and chilly, brooding was constant with both parents attending the chicks. During the night both parents brooded.

Hand-raising the Young

Judging from the large numbers of articles written on hand-raising infant greys, it appears that about as many greys are raised by surrogate human mothers as by their natural parents. No doubt some successful breeders of greys would prefer to hand-raise chicks because it is an established fact that hand-raised parrots, regardless of species, prove to be better talkers and more amiable pets than those raised by their natural parents.

Other breeders, however, are more or less forced to assume surrogate-mother roles because of problems with the natural parents of the chicks. Mrs. Wicks (1964), for example, was forced to remove a chick from the nest and hand-raise it. Her hen had successfully hatched all three of her eggs, but after three weeks one of the chicks died, and this death was followed four days later by the loss of a second chick. Mrs. Wicks ascribes these losses to the fact that the parents were "too young to cope with the responsibility of rearing a family to maturity." Unfortunately, Mrs. Wicks did not provide the age of the parent African greys.

Parental neglect does occur (Seth-Smith, 1939), and sometimes, as noted earlier, there is the danger of suffocation of the young nestlings (Dalton, 1957), particularly if the brood is large or the nesting site too small for both parents and their offspring. Sometimes, too, overzealousness on the part of an inexperienced and young hen can injure the young (Tavistock, 1929). There is also the possibility that for some reason or another, even though *Psittacus erithacus* mostly proves to be an attentive and loyal parent, the youngsters will be deserted (Lee, 1938-39). Fortunately, however, unlike many other species bred in captivity, there are no reports of nestlings found outside of the nest site.

Whatever the reason, when the nestlings are removed from the nest for hand-rearing, they usually should be less than three weeks old. Hand-rearing can be extremely demanding; the young must be fed regularly and consistently every two hours from dawn until about eleven at night. This regimen continues until the young are approximately seven or eight weeks old.

The diet must be prepared with the age of the young bird in mind. The food prepared should have a consistency not much thicker than milk.

Mrs. Wicks gave her seventeen-day-old Sukie, who was apparently very weak because of inadequate nourishment, a teaspoon of food every two hours. The formula consisted of Bengers and arrowroot mixed in hot milk so that it had the consistency of thin cream; it was continued until approximately the forty-fifth day. The mixture was then made thicker, and the youngster was introduced to shelled sunflower seeds and other more substantial and harder foods on a gradual basis. Apparently the youngster rapidly adjusted to the introduction of harder foods without difficulty, for in 1964 Mrs. Wicks wrote that by the fifty-third day, it "now enjoys a lamb-chop bone, with a little lean meat. *No fat.*"

Mrs. Hensel, (1978), an American who successfully hand-raised a brood of four from the time they were approximately two weeks old, fed them a "finely ground, blended mixture of dried foods mixed with warm water." Unfortunately, she did not specify what ingredients constituted her formula.

Gilbert Lee (1938-39), the very successful breeder and innovator who first raised greys in a barn loft, in returning to a conventional breeding program prepared the following formula:

> Use a double boiler to cook one part each of ground white corn, oats, barley, and with four times as much water, a pinch of powdered kelp. Use two large tablespoons of the mush, one half teaspoon of honey diluted with raw goat's milk or cow's milk—luke-warm it before feeding. The mixture should be rather thin as it must be remembered that this is the only moisture the bird gets.

Langberg (1958) fed his nestlings a gruel which consisted of milk, bread, glucose, vitamins and a product called "Recoven" which was reputedly rich in proteins.

Lee (1934) recommends cod-liver-oil with vitamins; this should be added to the prepared food mash.

The prepared mixture can be given to the youngster with either a syringe or a teaspoon which has had its edges bent to form a funnel shape. The syringe is usually inserted in the crop, but extreme care must be taken to avoid puncturing it. Many well-intentioned bird fanciers and aviculturists have inadvertently killed nestlings and fledglings in this manner. The spoon is the safest method; while it is somewhat slower and considerably messier, it will get the feeding done without mishap. The first attempt at feeding the youngster will be the most difficult, for the nestling must learn what it is to do in order to receive food. Simply insert the spoon under the mandible somewhat sideways, as the parent would do. The youngster will generally get the idea within a minute or two. The infant must be fed until the crop is *full* and *bulging*.

By the time the chick is seven to eight weeks old, it should be fed every four to five hours. Even then the youngster must be fed until its crop is full. After each feeding the beak should be wiped clean to prevent any accumulation of food on its beak and face, which could become a health hazard to the infant.

Weaning commences at approximately the ninth week. The bird is encouraged to become independent by the introduction of a food dish which is placed before it. A few seeds are sprinkled over the food mush. The youngster will usually telegraph its growing independence and its need to be weaned by occasionally refusing the mush which is offered, even though the bird's appropriate feeding time has been reached. This refusal, however, may also be a signal to the surrogate mother that soft foods are no longer acceptable. The mush must be made thicker. When the youngster refuses the food, food should again be offered within a half hour or so.

Some care must be exercised, however. A weaning youngster which is beginning to feed itself may not be getting a sufficient amount of food. Hand-feeding should accompany the youngster's attempt to feed itself until it is certain that the young bird is truly independent.

The change to harder foods must be made gradually. The proffered sunflower seeds must be shelled until the chick has learned to shell its own seeds. This can be done by cracking open the hull and giving the whole unit to the chick, the seed inside. As it learns to remove the kernel from the hull, it will also graduate to learn how to crack an intact hull to get at the contents.

Rearing by the Natural Parents

When a chick is fed by its natural parents, there is a considerable difference in the offspring's diet, as compared to the diet prepared by a surrogate mother. If conditions are appropriate, if the adult birds are fed properly and if they are loyal and faithful, then the food fed the offspring by the parents will obviously more than adequately meet the nutritional needs of the youngster.

The food offered by the parent birds has the consistency and color of milk because the food has been partially digested before it is regurgitated into the youngster's crop. Successful breeders who prefer that the natural parents raise their chicks always offer soaked seeds to the adult pair, a small matter in terms of the breeder's time but an important consideration in terms of the feeding process, for the pre-soaked seeds are more easily digestible for the adults and speed up the process by which the "milk" can be produced so that the youngsters do not remain hungry for any length of time. Various seeds are offered the parents: tapioca, maize, wheat, millet, safflower, hemp, canary, rice (boiled), sunflower seeds (shelled) and peanuts. The first-

African greys being held at an import facility.

time breeder will soon find that when dry seeds are offered with soaked seeds, the mated pair will invariably take the soaked seeds when there are youngsters in the nest.

Sufficient fresh water must always be available for the adults. Even though the soaked seeds already contain a quantity of water in them, the constant regurgitation in feeding the young draws a disproportionate amount of moisture out of the tissues. Much of the water that is drunk is mixed and released with the milk offered the youngsters.

Various fruits and greens should also be offered to the nesting pair. While some of these foods eventually end up in the milk, they are also essential to the adult's health during the caring for their young, when a great deal of energy is expended.

Growth Patterns

Information about the growth and development of *Psittacus erithacus* is scanty at best. Few breeders are prepared to succumb to their temptation to peer into a nest to study sitting, hatching, brooding or growth because of the danger that the youngsters may be abandoned by the parents. Their concern is well taken, for there is good reason to believe that the youngsters will be abandoned. The fact that the species is shy and retiring and that this tendency persists when they are tamed and in captivity should give sufficient basis for the suspicion of abandonment when there has been a disturbance or intrusion into the nest. Chapin (1939), for example, observed that after a climber scaled a towering tree to peer into the nesting cavity of a wild pair, the parents never returned to the nest, even though the "well incubated" eggs remained undisturbed. Five weeks later the nest still remained unoccupied, and it was subsequently claimed by a squirrel.

Because of these concerns, little is known about the development and growth of chicks in the natural state or of parental behavior in the nesting cavity. There is one report, however, of parental behavior in the handling of a chick.

One English breeder, Mr. E. Vane (1957), had a hen who, although there was no cock about, insisted on laying infertile eggs on at least two occasions. Concurrently, Vane had a pair of "yellow-cheeked Amazons" (yellow-faced Amazon, *Amazona xanthops*) which refused to tend to either their eggs or their hatched chicks, so that every clutch and brood was invariably lost. As it happened, the grey hen laid her infertile clutch shortly before a clutch was laid by the Amazon hen. Vane replaced the grey's infertile eggs with the clutch from the Amazon.

Interestingly enough, the African grey hen showed no particular annoyance or interest during the replacement process. When the foster eggs replaced her own infertile eggs, she immediately began brooding them until she successfully incubated one of them. When the chick began the difficult task of chipping away at its shell to release itself, the surrogate grey mother proceeded to help the infant by neatly chipping away the egg so that the shell fell into two pieces. Although the surrogate mother cleaned the infant, she did not feed it for twenty-four hours.

Whenever the grey had to move her foster offspring for one reason or another, she would bodily lift the infant by the head and gently deposit it at a more appropriate place of her choosing. *The infant was fed punctually every two hours.* For the first two weeks the baby was brooded constantly, except for brief intervals away from the nest. After the two-week period the intervals away from the nest became longer.

Again, unfortunately, there are few—indeed, very few—reports based on accurate observation of growth patterns and the attendant activities. The avicultural community, however, is fortunate that Mrs. Wicks maintained a diary on the one offspring that she was forced to foster into adulthood. Mrs. Wicks's account begins when the chick was already seventeen days old. She provides no information about the chick prior to that stage of development, but her observations after assuming her role as a foster mother provide considerable insight on the young African greys and their development. Her account, paraphrased and condensed, follows.

- September 25—17 days old, weighing 4.5 oz.: weak, fed every two hours; kept in dark box between feedings to protect eyes; hot-water bottle used as source of heat.
- October 1—23 days old, weighing 6 oz.
- October 6—26 days old, weighing 7.5 oz.: wing flapping; feet stomping.
- October 11—31 days old, weighing 9 oz.: began preening.
- October 16—36 days old, weighing 11.5 oz.: six teaspoons per meal; four meals per day.
- October 21—41 days old, weighing 13 oz.: red in tail showing; began eating shelled and crushed sunflower seeds.
- October 25—45 days old, weighing 14 oz.: shows signs

of tiring of baby food; wants shelled sunflowers.

- November 2 — 53 days old, weighing 15 oz.: uses beak to balance self; still tucks in at night, but perches during the day.
- November 5 — 56 days old, weighing 15 oz.: refuses all soft food.
- November 12 — 63 days old, weighing 13 oz.: cracks own seed; feathering; becoming independent.
- December 3 — 84 days old, weighing 13 oz.: flying already, but can't land well or change direction.
- December 10 — 91 days old, weighing 13 oz.: controls flight.
- December 24 — 15 weeks old, weighing 13 oz.: eyes beginning to "pearl."

Given the scarcity of published data on the growth and developmental patterns of *Psittacus erithacus,* a few other details may help to complete the picture presented by Mrs. Wicks. Greys reach fledging age a few days after other parrots, which fledge at eight weeks. The weaning period generally lasts into the sixth week, and full independence is reached by the thirteenth or fourteenth week. According to Dalton (1957), the young begin growing their head feathers during their seventh week. Smith (1968) reported that the young left the nest after approximately eighty days and that when they left their nest they were almost identical in appearance to their parents except for the fact that their eyes were almost black, their red tail feathers were tinged with brown on the underside and their gray appearance was somewhat darker than that of their parents. Within fourteen days the youngsters were feeding themselves completely.

Psittacus erithacus timneh. This African grey subspecies is not commonly available in the United States.

Psittacus erithacus timneh Fraser

Physical dimensions of *P. e. timneh*:
Wing: males, 206-223mm; females, 203-222mm
Tail: males, 75-83.5mm; females, 76-80mm
Culmen: males, 31-32.5mm; females, 30-31mm
Tarsus: males, 22-23.5mm; females, 23-25.5mm

Physical Description

The African grey varies significantly both in size and color over its vast territorial range. The eastern populations of this species tend to be larger than the western populations. Additionally, it has been observed that various local populations may be darker gray than other neighboring populations.

P. e. timneh, however, shows no significant color or size variances, and therefore it is considered a "good" subspecies of *P. e. erithacus*. Additionally, the Timneh is the smallest of the three currently recognized subspecies.

The most striking difference in appearance is the color of the tail which appears almost black from a short distance away, as compared to the almost vermilion shade of the other subspecies. The overall gray of the subspecies is significantly darker than that of the other subspecies.

Head Coloration: As with the other races of the African grey, the entire facial area is a grayish white. Beginning with the cere, this whitish area covers only the lower forehead, lores, upper-cheek and intermediate ear-covert areas. The remainder of the head area is a dark slate color, as opposed to the pale gray common to the other subspecies of *Psittacus erithacus*. The beak coloration is basically black, but the upper mandible is more reddish with its tip black. The iris is yellowish.

Body: The body plumage is a dark slate color, but the lower abdominal region and rump are a slightly lighter shade.

Wings: Similar to body and head colors. The primaries are black and the under wing-coverts a softer shade of gray.

Tail: The tail is primarily gray, uniform with the rest of the bird, with only two exceptions. One, the tail feathers are maroon colored, edged in brown. The color is so dark that descriptions of it range from brown, dark maroon, brown-maroon to dark red. Two, the under tail-coverts are dark gray tinged with dark red.

Feet: The feet and talons are black. The inner thighs are a lighter shade of gray than the outer thighs. The feet are slate gray to black.

Immatures: Almost identical to adults, except eyes are dark gray, almost black.

Geographic Distribution

As compared to the species as a whole, *P. e. timneh* has a comparatively limited territorial range. Initially it was believed that the Timneh's range was confined solely to Liberia, which is located in the extreme western portion of the species's range in Africa (Büttikofer, 1886). As a result of various field expeditions, it was found that the race was also common to Sherbro Island, Sierra Leone, but not as far westward as the capital of the country, Freeport, which is near the Sierra Leone-Guinea border (Kelsall, 1914). In 1921, the subspecies's most westerly range along the coast was redefined to be the Rokelle River in Sierra Leone (Lowe, 1921). The Timneh then appeared to be primarily confined to the tropical rain-forest region of Sierra Leone and Liberia.

In 1931, as a result of field studies conducted by Bates in the Nimba Mountain regions (which are found in the

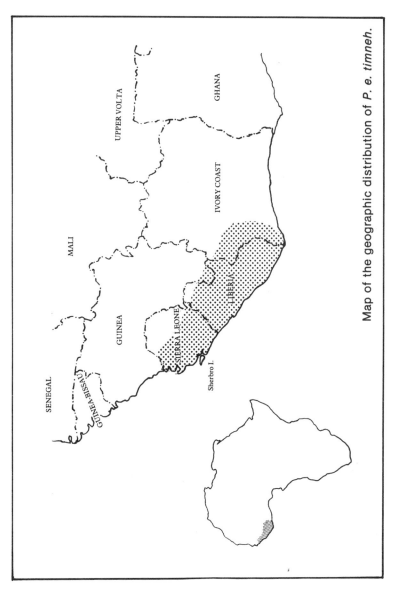

Map of the geographic distribution of *P. e. timneh*.

border area in the southeastern corner between Guinea and Sierra Leone), David Bannerman (1931) extended the Timneh's range northward to include southeastern Guinea. Subsequent field expeditions by Bannerman (1931) and Amadon (1953) have now indicated the Timneh's range to

A playpen-stand provides this pet African grey with a choice of foods and the opportunity for exercise.

also include the western tropical rain-forest regions of the Ivory Coast. It has not yet been established whether or not there is a line of intergradation between *P. e. timneh* and *P. e. erithacus,* which also inhabits the Ivory Coast. Also there are no reports of specimens collected which are intermediate between the two races.

P. e. timneh as a Cagebird

The Timneh, while not actually a rare subspecies, is not frequently imported into the United States; from that standpoint it may be described a "rare" bird. The exact reason for its lack of importation into the United States is uncertain, but it may be related to the race's overwhelming dark appearance, which in general is unbroken by any color of note. It is interesting that even during the last century in England, where African greys have always been popular, the only Timnehs to be seen were in zoological gardens. They are apparently unpopular there too; if they are not unpopular, they are certainly rarely imported.

While I have had no actual experience with the race, aside from having seen "broncos" (untamable birds) on various occasions, I have been informed on at least two occasions that the Timneh was not as fluent a talker as the other races of the African grey. As to whether this is true, I am unable to say, for while the two sources were knowledgeable about parrots, they were unable to substantiate this opinion of the Timneh with their own experience.

The truth probably is that the Timneh also proves to be a good talking parrot. But since the importers of exotic birds are primarily concerned with profits, the Timneh may be in their opinion a parrot which will not sell as readily as the other subspecies because of its lack of color. That may perhaps explain why, when the Timneh is offered for sale, its price is usually much lower than that of the other subspecies.

Psittacus erithacus erithacus. African greys are not difficult to tame, even though they do reveal a marked tendency to be indifferent to humans and a preference to maintain a social distance from their owners.

Psittacus erithacus erithacus Linné

Physical dimensions of *P. e. erithacus:*
Wing: males, 232-260mm; females, 232-255mm
Tail: males, 82-95mm; females, 80-95mm
Culmen: males, 32-37mm; females, 31-37mm
Tarsus: males, 26-28mm; females, 26-28mm

Physical Description

P. e. erithacus is easily identifiable: it is almost totally gray, except for its red tail. Depending on locality of origin, some specimens may be a darker shade of gray and/or larger than other specimens.

Head coloration:

Almost the entire head of *P. e. erithacus* is a soft, pastel gray except for the lores, lower forehead, cheeks and the intermediate regions of the ear-coverts just beyond the eye, which are a grayish white.

Body: The entire body, both breast and back regions, is also a soft, pastel shade of gray. The lower abdominal area is a slightly lighter shade. The faint white terminal margins of the breast feathers give the bird a scalloped appearance.

Wings: Uniformly gray as on the breast, back and head. The primaries are slate black.

Tail: The upper tail-coverts are also uniform in their grayness with the rest of the grey's plumage. The under coverts have a red tinge to them and the tail feathers are a bright red. The tail is stubby and short, more or less out of proportion with the other anatomical parts of the bird.

Feet: The feet are black. The inner thighs are a lighter shade of gray than the outer thighs.

Immatures: A young African grey looks almost identical to the adult. Once the young parrot is seven months or older, its eyes will have lost their blackness and the iris will have turned a straw-yellow color. While young specimens have generally less red to the tail, once the eye color has changed there is no assurance that the tail color can be relied upon for age determination because among adults there are variations between one individual and another in the extensiveness of red in the tail.

Geographic Distribution

P. e. erithacus occupies almost the entire range common to the species except for the most westerly region of Guinea, Sierra Leone, Liberia and western Ivory Coast. It is primarily found in the rain-forest belt of the African continent.

The most westerly extension of its range is in the eastern and central regions of the Ivory Coast. Extending eastward, the Ubangi River, which forms the boundary between Zaire and the Central African Republic, forms its most northerly extension in central Africa. Along the Atlantic coast, the range reaches through Nigeria, the Cameroons, Gabon and into northern Angola.

There has been some dispute concerning its most eastern extension. Most students of ornithology generally accept the southeastern shore of Lake Tanganyika in Tanzania as its most eastern region of occurrence. The same ornithologists also generally accept the northern and western shores of Lake Victoria, approximately 1,200 kilometers to the north, as the most northerly extent of its range. By defining the range this way, both western Kenya and Tanzania are included in the range, with the remote possibility that occasional flocks may be found in the most southeastern regions of the Sudan.

The eastern extent of its range seems to be primarily based on the conclusions arrived at by Chapin (1939) after examining reports of sightings in the region.

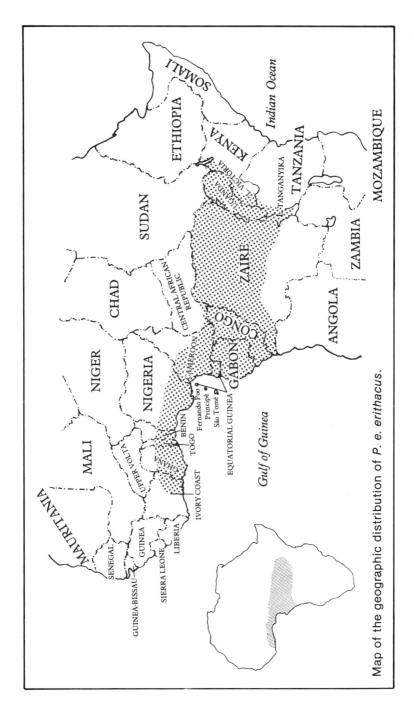

Map of the geographic distribution of *P. e. erithacus.*

In 1943, Moreau attacked this proposition by questioning the basis of Chapin's conclusions. He noted that Chapin relied on the Bangs and Loveridge (1933) paper in which a purported sighting of *Psittacus erithacus* was made at Kasanga in southeastern Tanzania. Moreau argued that the Chapin conclusion was in error because the sighting nearest to that location had taken place at Kasai in central Zaire, almost 1,200 km. to the west; the second nearest sighting was almost 800 kilometers to the north at Lake Kivu, the lake forming part of the international border between Zaire and Ruanda. If Moreau is correct, the most easterly range of *P. e. erithacus* is considerably west of Kenya and Tanzania. Not only are the western provinces of both these countries excluded from the range, but a significant portion of Zaire is also left out, and the Sudan becomes completely excluded from the range.

I am unable to resolve this dilemna, and the reader is left to his own devices as to whether Moreau's opinion is indeed correct. In the meantime, most current (popular) literature accepts the Chapin proposition that the species extends its range into Kenya and Tanzania.

In this connection, Mackworth-Praed and Grant (1952) believe that the range of *P. e. erithacus* is actually extending eastward. In this connection, however, these authors have failed to provide evidence for this conclusion or to cite other studies which could be examined to determine whether such conclusions can be safely drawn. Other students of ornithology such as Forshaw (1977) seem to have accepted this proposition based on the Mackworth-Praed and Grant assertion. If the range of the species is actually extending eastward, however, the reason may not necessarily be related to some inherent, instinctual characteristic common to the race as would be suggested by Mackworth-Praed and Grant.

While the African grey prefers the range common to the great equatorial forest, it is equally comfortable in the

African greys enjoy hanging upside down. *Psittacus erithacus* is somewhat unusual, for in the wild it prefers to climb from one place to another in a tree rather than fly or hop as most other parrot species do.

savanna terrains and cultivated areas. The species is captured and sold throughout significantly large regions outside of its natural habitat in Africa. For example, in 1870, Melliss observed that the African grey was a common captive parrot on the island of St. Helena, being imported from the western coast of Africa. Similarly, in 1893, on the eastern coast of Africa, Finn observed, the African grey was a "common household pet with Hindoos, Gandese and Europeans, being brought down from the interior." Since much of the eastern region of the continent has a climate similar to the central and western portions where the species is native, it is quite conceivable that sufficient numbers of the race have escaped to establish breeding populations which are more or less permanent in some localities. such small local populations, however, do not im-

Except for feeding and talking, most African greys are content to sit motionless. This pet grey, however, is certainly an exception to that rule; he enjoys doing his own version of the hornpipe.

ply an eastward expansion by the race, yet such sightings could suggest as much to field scientists who may observe the occasional individual in a region previously not considered part of the race's territorial habitat. Similarly, escaped caged birds could be mistaken as native to an area which has previously been unreported as part of the natural territory of the species. Such populations of escaped cage birds are completely isolated from the main territorial range of the race, and until evidence demonstrates otherwise they should be considered nothing more than isolated and temporary inhabitants.

P. e. erithacus as a Cagebird

The Jaco has been a popular parrot for several centuries. It is reported to have entertained the courts of Rome 2,000 years ago and to have been introduced to northern Europe in the sixteenth century during the bloom of the Renaissance.

Most African greys prefer to remain detached from involvement with human beings. Hand-feeding a pet grey may help to make it more sociable.

This trusting pet African grey permits handling.

While there are critics of the species, just as there are of any other, the African grey receives nothing but the highest of praise because of its ability to mimic. Even critics who may abhor the species for its color, shape or impersonality will readily concede that if the species is not the best, it certainly ranks among the top three best-talking species of parrots.

The stories about the African grey parrot are legion, and a book on anecdotes about the parrot could be written without much research or effort. Because it has been attributed with so many human qualities, one would expect it to be human. This view of the African grey, typical of those who perceive the species in anthropomorphic terms, was succinctly expressed by Henrietta Scheu (1936-37):

> These parrots . . . are not noisy and are such very
> good imitators of the human voice. Sometimes it
> is hard to distinguish his voice from one of the

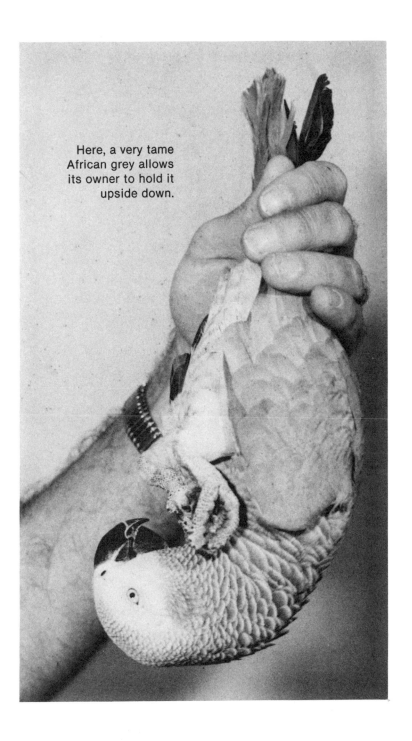

Here, a very tame African grey allows its owner to hold it upside down.

Most African greys can learn to do tricks, but often even trick-trained greys remain distant from their owners.

A pet grey "playing dead."

family and we find ourselves responding to his call, thinking it is some member of the family calling. He usually greets me in the morning with "hello, Mother" and from then on he talks the greater part of the day.

A disposition of subdued questions, accuracy in imitating what it hears in exact tone, pitch and intonation, and the uncanny appearance of intelligence are not only Mrs. Scheu's experience but also the opinion of most people who own a grey.

The Jaco is also a hardy parrot, not demanding much in special attention or care. There are numerous accounts of the race "enduring" the rigors of the kinds of winters that occur in northern Europe.

Finally, the Jaco is a gentle being. It is a rare African grey which does not accept taming and which, once tamed, will bite people, even after being provoked. This race comes with excellent credentials.

There are some, however, who find fault with the race's coloring and because of its anatomy, it suggests to them a "snaky," vulture-like appearance. It appears to me that such claims are purely subjective and not really pertinent to the character and personality of the race.

Of more serious concern, however, is the contention that the Jaco rarely enters into a relationship which could be described as a reciprocal relationship with people. Relationships with parrots can be classified into three types: (1) parrots which are trained but will never accept any other relationship with humans, (2) parrots which are tame (and even trained to do "tricks") but never enter into any relationships with people, and (3) parrots which (along with being tamed and trained) *prefer* to be with people. While the term "pet" can be applied to all of these three types, the term really has relevance only in consideration with the last option.

A pet parrot, then, is one which enjoys human companionship, which seeks it out and which is at its best only when it is with people. Unfortunately, the African grey rarely fits this last category. While African greys are rarely vicious with people, an admirable and desirable quality in itself, they are almost always "standoffish," aloof and distant.

This personality characteristic of the race is closely associated with the other major criticism directed at the race: it lacks a colorful personality. The Jaco is content to remain by itself for hours on end and, except for feeding and talking, most of the time it is motionless. It is, according to critics, something to hear from time to time, but mostly it is something which never does anything more than sit.

Yet this behavior in itself may be a virtue, particularly for those pet owners who prefer to remain detached and have no contact with their birds and who object to the noise and antics characteristic of many other parrot species.

Psittacus erithacus princeps
Boyd Alexander

Physical dimensions of *P. e. princeps:*
Wing: males, 227-250mm; females, 225-250mm
Tail: males, 100-114mm; females, 85-105mm
Culmen: males, 34.5-39mm; females, 32-40mm
Tarsus: males, 26-27.5mm; females, 25-26mm

Physical Description

P. e. princeps is considered identical in all ways to *P. e. erithacus* except that it is alleged to be larger and to be a darker-plumaged subspecies. The status of the Princeps as a qualified subspecies is seriously questioned by numerous ornithologists, for, as noted above and elsewhere, the size and color differences exhibited by this race can be found throughout the entire territorial range of *P. e. erithacus,* particularly in the eastern populations of the species.

P. e. princeps as a Subspecies

Boyd Alexander originally classified *Psittacus erithacus* as a distinct subspecies on the basis of the color found on the island specimens, which he considered darker, and the size, which he believed was larger than the immediate mainland types.

In 1914, after Alexander's death, David A. Bannerman made some interesting observations about the Alexander collection of specimens which had been used to substantiate the subspecific status of the race. Bannerman remeasured all of the skins and found discrepancies in measurements; both male and female skins proved to be actually larger than what Alexander had recorded! While the second set of measurements would seem to support Alexander's original argument even that much more conclusively, Bannerman also observed that specimens collected in Uganda were at least as large, if not larger in some cases, than the Principé Island specimens. He additionally observed that while the *princeps* were darker in appearance than usual, "it must be remembered that birds from the mainland often exhibit considerable variation in this respect." Bannerman, however, did not totally reject Alexander's classification, for he tempered his analysis by suggesting that subsequent studies would probably prove that there are several other races of the species still to be discovered.

Bannerman's analysis no doubt had considerable influence over subsequent study and controversy. Stigand, for example, while quite precise in his discussion on *erithacus* and *timneh,* hedges on whether or not *princeps* is another subspecies by curtly noting that *"Psittacus erithacus princeps,* which comes from the Gulf of Guinea, Prince's Island and Fernando Poo, is by some naturalists considered to be a subspecies . . ." While various other students of ornithology such as Mackworth-Praed and Grant (1952), Snow (1950), David Bannerman (1953) and others have accepted the status of *princeps* as established in 1909, Amadon (1953) was to raise the issue again:

> Aside from the slight size variation mentioned, uniformity prevails. I am unable to see that the birds of São Tomé and Principe are darker than the mainland ones, when allowance is made for the condition of the plumage. The light gray bloom of the plumage of this parrot is easily lost by wear, either in the wild or during the skinning process. Island birds in fresh plumage are well matched in color by specimens from southern Nigeria and elsewhere on the mainland . . .

I make no pretense of even attempting to resolve the issue of the true geographical distribution of *princeps* or whether or not *princeps* is actually a subspecies. The issue seems strongly contaminated by personal interpretation of color variations and by the problems presented in interpreting data involving size variations of specimens from one region to another.

The debate appears to remain unresolved, and even though there are some sources which include *princeps* as a classified and accepted subspecies, others in listing *princeps* make note that its status is questionable.

I have had only one opportunity to see a live specimen purported to be a *princeps*. I was unable to note any significant differences from specimens of *P. e. erithacus* in either size or color.

Geographic Distribution

There is also a considerable amount of confusion concerning the actual range of *P. e. princeps*. Most sources restrict the race to Principé, an island approximately 150 square kilometers in size and approximately 300 kilometers from the nearest mainland, which is Equatorial Guinea. Other contemporary authorities, however, such as Forshaw (1977), have included the island of Fernando Poo in *princeps's* range. Fernando Poo is situated approximately 300 kilometers northeast of Principé, and only about 75 kilometers from the mainland, its nearest point being the Cameroons. This difference in understanding what constitutes the exact range of the race can be traced to the earliest sightings of *princeps* and the difficulties encountered in classifying *princeps* because of interpretations concerning size and color.

Historically, the first European to make extensive notes of the African greys on the islands concerned was Keulemans, who wrote about the species on the island of

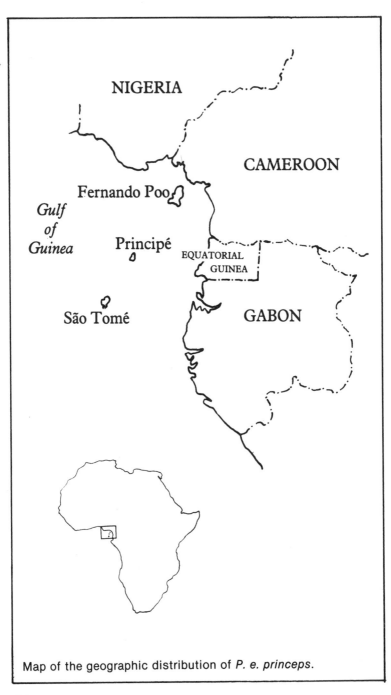

Map of the geographic distribution of *P. e. princeps*.

Principé in 1865. Because there was so little known about the species at the time, Keulemans appears fascinated by the species and studied it in detail, for as he was to later recollect: "I daily observed their habits and mode of life in the wild state" (Greene, 1887). While his notes on the African grey appear to be substantial (Greene devotes several pages to direct quotations from Keulemans's notes), Keulemans appears not to have observed any differences between the island and the mainland populations. This is an important consideration, for Keulemans was, judging from his writings, an individual concerned with details.

In 1903, Boyd Alexander was in the Gulf of Guinea area and was on Fernando Poo for some time. He was to write that he had observed numerous large flocks of African greys flying quite high overhead and that *they were migrants to the island.* That same year, Salvadori (1903) travelled throughout the Gulf of Guinea islands studying the avifauna and noting general observations on minor differences between island and mainland types. Salvadori was an outstanding ornithologist in his day. Apparently what differences he did note while on the islands did not constitute a significant departure from other *P. erithacus* populations.

The next mention of *Psittacus erithacus* in the Gulf of Guinea area occurred in 1909. Alexander had again returned to the islands. After studying the avifauna at São Tomé for a month, he took a steamer to Annabon where he did further work and then travelled on to Principé, about which he wrote in a letter to *The Ibis,* April 9, 1909:

> You will be surprised to hear that the Parrot on that island [Principé] is quite distinct from *Psittacus erithacus*—in fact I might almost describe it as a black parrot. I am sending home the description of it, and propose to call it *P. princips.*

Another letter from Alexander was published in *The British Ornithological Club Bulletin* in 1909. The entire text is quoted below:

A typical African grey activity—sitting motionless.

Mr. Boyd Alexander forwarding the following description of a new species of Parrot from Prince's Island, West Africa:

PSITTACUS PRINCEPS, sp. n.

Adult male and female: Similar to *P. erithacus,* Linn., but larger and darker. Entire upper and under parts very dark grey, almost blackish; feathers, especially of the underparts, edged with dark blue, giving the bird when viewed in certain lights the appearance of being strongly washed with inky blue.

Male: Wing 235-238mm.; tail 100-114.

Female: Wing 230-235mm; tail 105.

Hab. Prince's Island, W. Africa.

After the work sojourn on Principé, Alexander then went on to Fernando Poo and then eventually to the African mainland. While on Fernando Poo, Alexander studied the avifauna just as he had done in 1903. However, *neither of the letters which had been written to the* B.O.C.B. *and* The Ibis *made any mention of there being particular similarities between both island populations which distinguished them as uniquely alike – and distinctly different from mainland types!*

Bannerman was to write an article on Alexander's collection in 1914 after Alexander's death. After reviewing some of the history related to the classification of *princeps,* he then quoted a brief passage from a book entitled *Boyd Alexander's Last Journey,* which had been published by Alexander's brother. The book had apparently been prepared from the contents of Alexander's diaries. In discussing *princeps,* again, only the island of Principé is mentioned. Alexander had not considered the Fernando Poo population of African greys a *princeps* race.

In his review of *Psittacus erithacus princeps,* Bannerman concluded by writing that *"I cannot separate birds from Fernando Poo from specimens from Prince's Island"* [emphasis mine]. He was in fact saying both populations were one and the same. From that point on it appears that while Alexander had restricted the race to Principé Island, future publications were to include Fernando Poo in the territorial range of *princeps.*

From Bannerman's comment there can be some confusion as to his intent. It will be recalled that Bannerman had earlier noted that *princeps* was in his judgment similar to various eastern populations of *P. erithacus* which also proved to be darker and larger. While he had not rejected the possibility that the gulf island populations were indeed a separate race, it is clear that he had deep reservations concerning such a classification. It is not clear, however, whether Bannerman was in effect saying that since there is no difference between the two island populations and because Fernando Poo specimens were like the mainland populations, thus *de facto* a subspecies does not exist. It

This African grey, named Smokey, lies on his back and chews a piece of rawhide. While lying on the back is not a particularly unusual trick, Smokey enjoys it; he not only will lie on his back in his own cage without encouragement from household members, but he will also do so for several minutes at a time when playing with his rawhide.

Opposite:
This is a young adult African grey, *Psittacus e. erithacus*. It is obviously a gentle pet.

Fresh air and sunshine are fine for a pet parrot, but unless its wing(s) is clipped, the bird is likely to fly away.

may be that in the interim between Alexander's classification and Bannerman's own 1914 publication, additional studies which clearly included the Fernando Poo population in the *princeps* subspecies had been conducted.

The problem of whether *princeps* actually includes greys of both islands may be a problem resulting from any one of several other sources. It may very well be that Salvadori's description of *princeps* coincided so closely with Alexander's that Chapin (1939) and perhaps other (presently unidentified) authorities considered both populations as being one and the same. The probability of the two being the same subspecies is unlikely, however, for the two islands in question are almost 300 kilometers apart. While the island of Principé is 300 km. from the mainland and its isolation thereby favors the evolution of characteristics which would be unique to its population, Fernando Poo is only 75 or so kilometers from the mainland, close enough to favor migration and exchange of mainland Fernando Poo populations. Additionally, it is highly unlikely that two separate islands 300 kilometers apart would have a species of bird life evolving identical characteristics or that, given the considerable distance separating the islands, particularly when Fernando Poo is so close to the mainland, an exchange of populations between the two islands would take place.

P. e. princeps as a Cagebird

As there are only minor differences between *P. e. princeps* and *P. e. erithacus* (if in fact *princeps* is a distinct race), it is doubtful there would be any specific personality differences between the two races. Repeating the professional opinions and attitudes concerning *princeps* would be redundant at this point; the reader is encouraged to read over the appropriate section on *P. e. erithacus*.

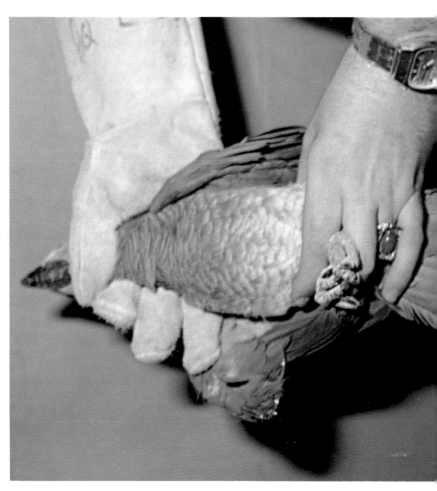

This African grey is being held for examination. Note the ease in which the chest, feet, under wings, head and eyes can be checked without the risk of the bird being injured or the examiner being bitten.

Opposite:
An African grey being hand-tamed. Greys do not have mean dispositions, and while they growl a great deal—particularly when wild and being tamed— they rarely inflict nasty bites.

103

Bibliography

Alexander, Boyd. 1903. On the birds of Fernando Poo. *The Ibis* 45:330-403.

_____. 1908-09. Letter to the editor, *The British Ornithological Club Bulletin* 23:74.

_____. 1909. Letter to the editor, *The Ibis* 5:564-5.

Amadon, Dean. 1953. Avian systematics of evolution in the Gulf of Guinea. *Bulletin of the American Museum of Natural History* 100(3):397-451.

Bangs, O. and Loveridge, A. 1933. Reports on the scientific results of an expedition to the southwestern highlands of Tanganyika. *Bulletin of the Harvard Museum of Comparative Zoology* 75:143-221.

Bannerman, David A. 1914. Reports on the birds collected by the late Mr. Boyd Alexander (Rifle Brigade) during his last expedition to Africa, part 1. *The Ibis* 2:596-631.

_____. 1931. Account of the birds collected by Mr. G. L. Bates on behalf of the British Museum in Sierra Leone, French Guinea. *The Ibis* 73:666-97.

_____. 1953. Birds of west equatorial Africa, vol. 1. Edinburgh: Oliver and Boyd.

Boosey, Edward. 1945. The breeding of African grey parrots at Kensington. *Avicultural Magazine,* 5th series, 10:147-50.

_____. 1950. The Kensington Foreign Bird Farm comes of age. *Avicultural Magazine* 56:252-63.

_____. 1952-53a. Letter to the editor, *Avicultural Magazine* 58-59:114.

_____. 1952-53b. Letter to the editor, *Avicultural Magazine* 58-59:150.

Büttikofer, J. 1886. Zoological researches in Liberia. *The Ibis* 28:80.

Chapin, F.M. 1939. The birds of the Belgian Congo, part II. *Bulletin of the American Museum of Natural History* 175:1-632.

Dalton, K.W. 1957. Breeding of Timneh x African grey parrots. *Avicultural Magazine* 63:199.

Editorial note, *Aviculture*, 1945, 342.

Finn, F. 1893. Notes on birds observed during a collecting expedition to eastern Africa. *The Ibis* 35: 223-234.

Forshaw, Joseph M. 1977. *Parrots of the world.* Neptune, New Jersey: T.F.H. Publications.

Greene, W. T. 1884-87. *Parrots in captivity.* Neptune, New Jersey: T.F.H. Publications, 1977.

Hensel, Mickey. 1978. Four for four—most unusual. *American Cage-Bird Magazine*, May 1978, 24-25.

Kelsall, H. J. 1914. Notes on a collection of birds from the Sierra Leone. *The Ibis*, 10th series, 192-228.

Langberg, Walther. 1958. Successful breeding of African grey parrots in Denmark. *Avicultural Magazine* 64:57-64.

Lee, Gilbert. 1930. Breeding the grey parrot twenty-seven years ago. *Aviculture* 2:255-57.

———. 1934. Breeding the African grey talking parrot. *Aviculture* 5:18.

———. 1935. Advertisement, *Aviculture*, inside cover.

———. 1938-39. Hand-rearing grey parrots. *Aviculture* 8-9:117.

———. 1955. Advertisement, *Aviculture*, inside cover.

Lister, U. G. 1962. African grey parrots in captivity. *Nigerian Field* 27:127-34.

Lowe, W. P. 1921. The birds of Iasso and adjoining islands of the Rokelle River, Sierra Leone. *The Ibis* 63:265-82.

———. 1937. Report on the Lowe-Waldron expeditions to

In addition to its basic diet of seeds, an African grey should also be offered fruit and green food.

This particular African grey, believe it or not, is totally wild. Throughout the entire photo session it growled but nevertheless remained on Scott Smith's arm. About a second before this photograph was taken, the grey took a nip at Scott's finger—for which he admonishes it.

the Ashanti forests and northern territories of the Gold Coast. *The Ibis* 79:635-62.

Mackworth-Praed, C. W. and Grant, C. H. B. 1952. *Birds of east and northwestern Africa*, vol. I. Toronto: Longmans, Green and Co.

Marchant, S. 1942. Some birds of the Owerri Province, South Nigeria. *The Ibis* 84:137-96.

Melliss, J. C. 1870. Notes on the birds of the Island of St. Helena. *The Ibis* 12:97-107.

Moreau, R. E. 1943. A contribution to the ornithology of the east side of Lake Tanganyika. *The Ibis* 85:397.

The nest box. 1943. *Aviculture* 13:15.

News and views. 1960. *Avicultural Magazine* 66:81.

Salvadori, T. 1903. Ornithologia Golfo de Guinea. *Bocage, Jorn. Sci. Lisboa* 1903:8-46.

Scheu, Henrietta. 1936-37. Birds as pets. *Aviculture* 6-7: 40-41.

Serle, W. 1957. A contribution to the ornithology of the eastern region of Nigeria. *The Ibis* 99:372-418.

_____. 1965. A third contribution to the ornithology of the British Cameroons. *The Ibis* 107:60-94.

Seth-Smith, David. 1939. The early years of the Avicultural Society. *Avicultural Magazine*, 5th series, 4:327-31.

Sharpe, R. Bowdler. 1907. On further collections of birds from the Efulen district of Cameroon, West Africa. *The Ibis*, 9th series, 49:426-64.

Smith, Clifford. 1968. Five years with African greys. *Avicultural Magazine* 74:13-14.

Snow, D. W. 1950. The birds of São Tomé and Principé in the Gulf of Guinea. *The Ibis* 92:579-95.

Someren, V. G. van. 1916. A list of birds collected in Uganda and British East Africa, with notes on their nesting and other habits. *The Ibis* 4:193-252.

Tavistock. 1929. Notes on the 1929 Season. *Avicultural Magazine*, 4th Series, 7:233-40.

Vane, E. N. T. 1957. Rearing the Yellow-Cheeked Amazon. *Avicultural Magazine* 63:183-88.

Wicks, Eve. 1964. Sukie—baby Africa grey parrot. *Avicultural Magazine* 70:155-57.

Young, Charles C. 1946. Notes on some birds of the Cameroon Mountain district. *The Ibis* 88:348-82.

A pair of African greys resting on the highest perch in the aviary.

Opposite:
Smokey listens intently as Dave Schuelke, of Garden Grove, California, whistles a brief tune. For several months, Smokey refused even to attempt mimicry. Now he has decided to also begin talking.

Because African grey parrots are not sexually dimorphic, sexing is best accomplished by laboratory or surgical procedures.

Diagnostic Laparoscopy in Birds

William C. Satterfield, D.V.M.

What is laparoscopy?

Laparoscopy is a procedure for examining the spaces within the body without major surgical invasion of those spaces. The laparoscope is an instrument developed over twenty years ago for use in human medicine. Since the late 1960's, the miniaturized laparoscope—which employs a fiberoptic system—and accompanying instruments have been used by physicians in procedures such as examination of the unborn fetus and the knee in humans. Application of the laparoscope to bird sexing came in the earliest phase of its veterinary use.

Light from a remote source of illumination travels through a small, flexible, glass-filled tubing to a viewing tip with an eyepiece. The light level is adjustable to allow the veterinarian to select the best illumination for the procedure. Most laparoscopes contain a magnification system which enlarges the final image up to thirty times, allowing close-up, detailed examination of the surface of the organs. Viewing tips are available in various sizes, but avian laparoscopy is often done with a 2.2 mm diameter (14-gauge) tip, which is about the size of a large hypodermic needle.

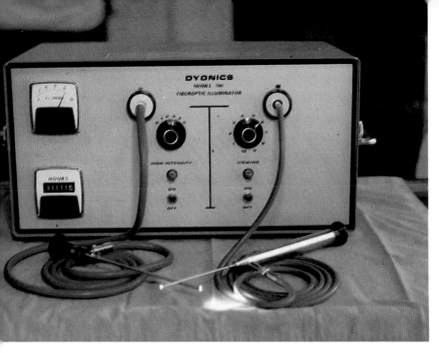

Above: Dual light source for the laparoscope. The light controls on the left are for photography, the controls on the right for general examining use. *Below:* Portable light source with laparoscope, cannula, and trochars.

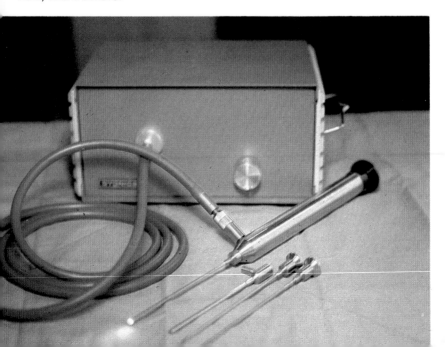

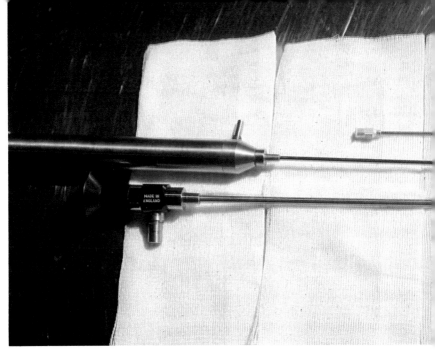

Above: Two laparoscopes compared for diameter with a 16-gauge hypodermic needle. *Below:* Laparoscope with attachment for needle biopsy. The biopsy needle enters a special side port of the cannula.

Why are birds laparoscoped?

Birds are laparoscoped to determine their sex and breeding condition, to examine the internal organs for signs of disease, and to take small tissue samples for microscopic study. In sexually monomorphic species (those in which the male and female show no external differences) laparoscopy is the most common procedure for sex determination. With the world population of all wild animals decreasing rapidly and with federal regulations restricting the importation of many species, captive breeding programs have become increasingly important. Pairing birds of confirmed sex and in good breeding condition can be the most important key to a successful avian propagation program.

Procedure for sex determination by laparoscopy

For most species, an assistant restrains the bird manually on its right side by holding the wings together over the back and gently extending the legs. If anesthesia is used, a se-

Positioning of a bird is accomplished by holding its wings together over its back and extending its legs slightly posteriorly.

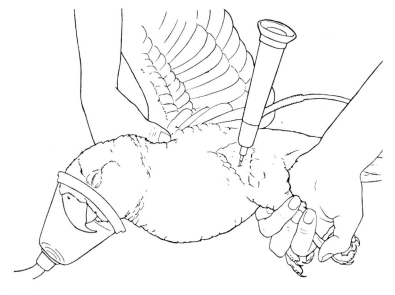

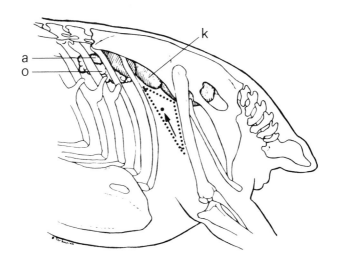

The landmarks for locating the optimum area for introducing the cannula are the last rib, the ilium, and the proximal half of the shaft of the femur. The approximate site is marked by the arrow and dot. *a*, adrenal; *o*, gonad; *k*, kidney.

cond assistant monitors the bird's breathing and heart rate.

A small skin area on the bird's left side is prepared for sterile surgery. The landmarks for locating the optimum area for the procedure are the last rib, the ilium, and the proximal half of the femur. Within the triangle formed by these, a small incision is carefully made through the skin and superficial muscle. This is no more traumatic than giving a hypodermic injection and generally produces no noticeable discomfort to the bird. The hollow sleeve, or *cannula*, containing a sharp pointed rod, the *trochar*, is inserted into the abdominal air sac. The trochar is then removed from the cannula, and the viewing tip of the laparoscope with its light-carrying bundles and optical system is inserted. For birds weighing less than 100 grams, the laparoscope may be inserted directly through the incision without using the cannula, which reduces the diameter of the instrument to 1.7 mm.

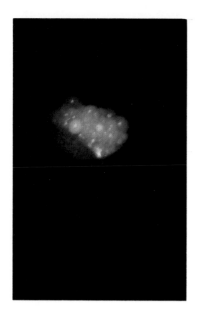
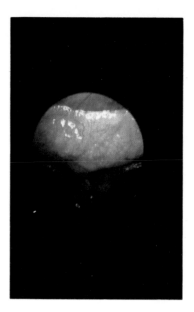

Above, left: inactive ovary of an amazon parrot—note undeveloped follicles. *Right:* Immature ovary of a young amazon parrot. *Below, left:* Ovary of a parrot, showing a developing follicle. *Right:* Ovary of a parrot, with a more mature follicle.

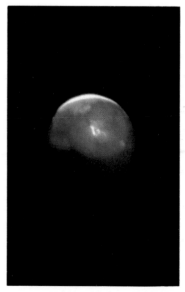

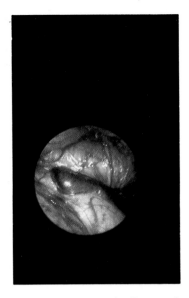

Above, left: The white organ in the center is the testicle of a Crowned Crane. *Right:* The dark organ has the normal color of a testicle of a Glossy Ibis. *Below, left:* The white organ in the center is a mature, active testicle of an African Grey Parrot. *Right:* Tuberculosis lesions in the liver of a turaco.

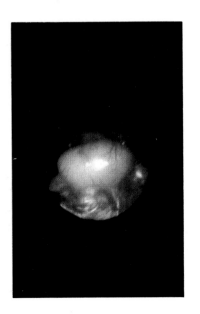

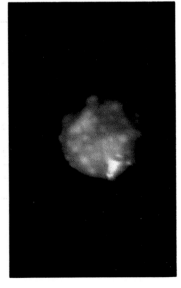

When properly placed, the viewing tip of the laparoscope will be near the anterior (uppermost) lobe of the left kidney, and the gonad will be seen just above this point, attached to the adrenal gland. Identification of the gonad is completed in about one minute, and the laparoscope and cannula are withdrawn. A topical antibiotic powder is placed on the small puncture; sutures are not required.

Whether the examination is done in a veterinary hospital or at an aviary, the laparoscopic equipment is thoroughly cleaned and sterilized before each bird is examined so there is no danger of infection. Liquid or gas sterilization is used since steam-and-heat sterilization is damaging to the lens system of the laparoscope.

What does the veterinarian see when a bird is laparoscoped?

The ovary in a female bird is a cluster of hundreds of round follicles, each containing an undeveloped ovum. A young bird will have relatively small, uniform follicles. A female bird in breeding condition will show a large developing follicle or a mature follicle just prior to ovulation and egg formation.

The male bird has a smooth, dense testicle, either pale or dark. The veterinarian can evaluate the bird's breeding condition by the size of the testicle and its blood supply. Development and activity of the gonads can be correlated with behavioral data to indicate the bird's response to environmental, nutritional, and husbandry conditions.

Are there other ways of determining the bird's sex?

In waterfowl and poultry, *vent sexing* remains one of the most useful and rapid techniques for sexing newly hatched young. Many aviculturists effectively utilize this easy-to-learn method. However, there are many other avian species for which this technique is not effective. In these species, aviculturists have paired birds "naturally" by behavioral characteristics. Unfortunately, there is room for error in this method, and many individuals have been paired with another of the same sex.

A modification of the caponizing procedure (*laparotomy*) has been used in various ways to allow direct visualization of the gonads via a small incision and the use of an otoscope or small speculum. This is an effective technique, but it has not gained wide acceptance because size of the surgical incision is relatively large and its application is limited to sexing.

Two nonsurgical techniques for sexing monomorphic birds include *sex chromosome determination* and *fecal steroid analysis*. Both procedures involve a uniquely equipped laboratory and are quite expensive and time consuming. Until recently, fecal steroid laboratory services have been limited primarily to endangered species in large collections, but are now commercially available through local veterinarians in the U.S.

Are there other uses for avian laparoscopy?

In addition to its use in sex determination, laparoscopy is a versatile diagnostic tool. The air sacs and posterior surface of the lungs may be examined for signs of infection. The kidneys, adrenals, spleen, intestines, and liver may be rapidly evaluated visually, and samples taken for bacteriologic culture or histopathologic study under the microscope. Information about the bird's health is available in a short time without major surgery.

An increasingly common procedure is the liver biopsy. Biopsy results can be of major assistance to the manager of a large or valuable collection that has had a problem with avian tuberculosis, viral hepatitis, amyloidosis, or an inclusion-body disease. This technique can provide rapid and accurate answers about the status of an individual bird without endangering its health, and the manager can use this information to select birds for quarantine or entry into the collection.

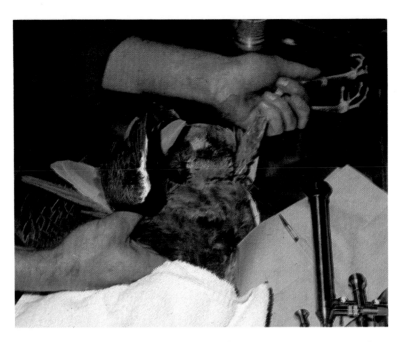

Above: A night-heron being prepared for sexing. *Below:* A Nicobar Pigeon is laparoscoped for sex.

Right: An immature night-heron placed on its back for diagnostic liver biopsy to test for avian tuberculosis. *Below, left:* The small piece of tissue in the palm is the sample taken from the liver. *Below, right:* Placement of a single catgut suture in the skin of the night-heron after biopsy.

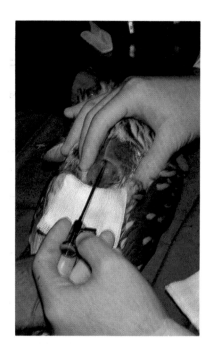

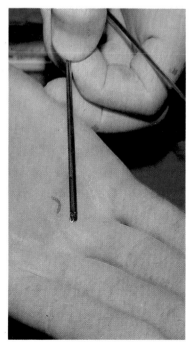

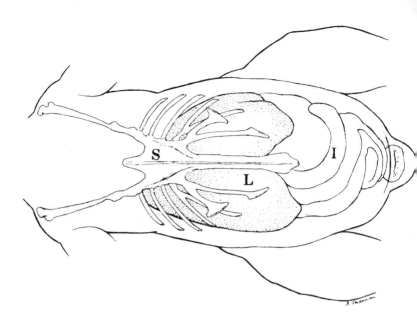

Above: Topography of the vental skeleton and superficial viscera. *L,* liver; *S,* sternum; *I,* intestine. *Below:* Lateral topography with the needlescope inserted for examination of the liver.

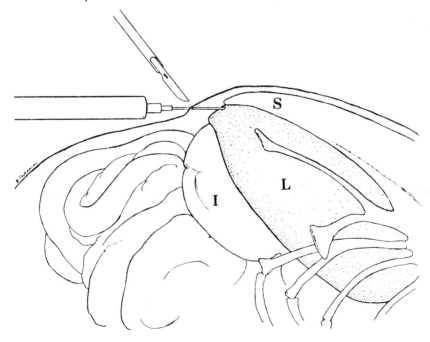

When the liver is to be examined, the bird is placed on its back with its feet held back. The laparoscope with a biopsy attachment is inserted through the abdominal tissue directly behind the sternum in the midline. The surgeon can view most surfaces of the liver and can even examine the heart in some cases. If abnormal tissue is seen on the surface of the liver, the surgeon can take a small portion of this tissue to be sent to the laboratory for microscopic examination. The laparoscope is withdrawn, and a topical antibiotic is placed on the small skin wound. A single suture may sometimes be placed in the skin.

Conclusion

Laparoscopy, one of the major recent advances in the science of avian medicine, is an important conservation and husbandry technique and diagnostic tool. It is a rapid, safe, noninjurious procedure that allows direct visual observation of the gonads and examination and sampling of the abdominal organs in a living bird. Used as an adjunct to other techniques, laparoscopy has significant applications in the management and conservation of avian species in captivity.

Supplemental Reading

Bush, M.; Wildt, D. E.; Kennedy, S.; and Seager, S. W. J. 1978. Laparoscopy in zoological medicine. *JAVMA* 173:1081-1087.

Czekala, N. M., and Lasley, B. L. 1977. A technical note on sex determination in monomorphic birds using faecal steroid analysis. *Inter. Zoo Yearbook* 17:209-211.

Harrison, G. J. 1978. Endoscopic examination of avian gonadal tissue. *Vet. Med./Small Animal Clinics* 73:479-484.

McIlwaith, C. W., and Fessler, J. F. 1978. Arthroscopy in the diagnosis of equine joint disease. *JAVMA* 172:263-268.

Satterfield, W. C. 1980. Diagnostic laparoscopy in birds. In *Current Veterinary Therapy VII*, ed. R. W. Kirk. Philadelphia: W. B. Saunders Co.